A monkey ate my breakfast

Motorhome adventures in Morocco

Julie and Jason Buckley

ACKNOWLEDGEMENTS

This book wouldn't have been possible without the unending love and support of our families, who never questioned our sanity when we quit our 'normal' lives and set off on our adventure.

A big thanks goes to Chris and Tina for their fab companionship and last, but no way least, a huge debt of gratitude to JT and Josh for their aching eyes and proof-reading skills.

ISBN: 1481819704
ISBN-13: 978-1481819701

CONTENTS

INTRODUCTION

Quitting our jobs in the summer of 2011 was a big step. With the UK in the middle of what seemed like an unending recession, friends told us we were brave, but we weren't sure if we were actually being foolish. We'd lived in Nottingham, in the middle of England, for almost 40 years, and the past twenty odd years had been spent working our way up respective career ladders. We'd been saving up for our trip for a couple of years and in August 2011 we realised we had enough in the pot for a year on the road. Our plan, if you can call it that, was simply to potter around Europe in Dave, our 19 year old motorhome.

The thought of going to Africa never crossed our minds, why would it? Charlie, our Cavalier King Charles Spaniel and surrogate son, was coming with us. The EU pet passport scheme was unclear if he'd be allowed back into the UK should he venture to such an exotic place, so we didn't give Africa a second thought. After all Europe is a big enough place.

On the 12th of October 2011 we sailed across the channel to begin our adventure. As we made our way down through France, across Northern Spain and into Portugal we felt fear and joy with the challenges we faced on the road. We learned much about ourselves, met like-minded travellers and formed lasting friendships.

Sitting in the sunshine at a friend's villa in Portugal's Algarve (even on an adventure, you still need a break) we learned that the pet passport scheme would change on the 1st of January 2012. The doors to Africa were now open to us. Fellow travellers Chris and Tina, and their pooch Loli, were in Spain and heading for the ferry; it was too good an opportunity to miss.

With no experience of the Islamic world, except that presented by BBC correspondents on a TV in the background of our previous lives, we were thankfully unprepared for what was to come. *"You'll either love it or hate it"* was the generic message we got from the people we read about or met who had journeyed there in a motorhome.

Upon entering the country our initial reaction was, as we'd been warned, to turn around and leave. Suddenly we were rich. What we'd previously seen as our decrepit, yellow-skinned motorhome morphed into a luxury rolling hotel. We became unwilling centres of attention. People, with no apparent purpose, stood along isolated sections of road and stared at us, some waving or pointing. We were, unwittingly, pulled over by a drug dealer in his 4x4 and the bundle of fur that is Charlie the pooch fascinated the local children. Some screamed and fell backwards as he padded around a corner, the braver boys demonstrated their courage with a quick grab or stroke.

Our skin and clothes indelibly marked us out as foreigners and we became used to a steady stream of requests to look at goods, or buy some service or other. After a while the distraught faces pulled by children when we refused their unending requests for *Dirhams* (money) or *bonbons* (sweets), hurt less. Although we had known we would see poverty, it was undeniably a shock to see men struggling with twisted wooden ploughs, and children shepherding tiny bedraggled flocks of sheep and goats.

During our time in the country we slowly became more at ease. We wound our way south through brick-red gorges, past families playing with sleds and broken skis on snow-covered mountains, through the dirty dust of deserts to the edge of the Sahara and back again. Fez amazed us. Marrakech annoyed us. Essaouira chilled us out. Tangier, which we'd avoided through sheer fear on our way into the country, proved tame on our return.

We've relished reliving our adventure while writing this book, visiting places and meeting people twice. Fasten your seatbelt and join us in Dave the motorhome. Bounce along rough roads dodging donkeys and tuck your elbows in as the Grand Taxis and lorries rush past. Cross your fingers that Dave doesn't snap a wheel off and immerse your senses in the exotic, bustling towns and cities of Morocco. Come and feel the elation.

GETTING IN

The little shop sat in the middle of an industrial estate dwarfed by cubed, metal buildings. The only sign that it was the right place came from an international collection of white motorhomes parked across the street. It wasn't a secret, but you have to ask around to find out about it. It was the place to buy tickets to North Africa.

Among the motorhoming community there seemed to be unwritten rules about how it was done. We'd tried to deduce these by reading internet articles, travellers blogs and forums, and chatting with folks we'd met along the way. The first stage, a rather obvious one, as all attempts to build a bridge or tunnel had failed, was to buy a ferry ticket. We needed to buy passage for ourselves, our pooch Charlie, and our ageing three tonne wagon of a motorhome, Dave, who we named after the previous owner's cat. That wasn't even the cat's name, but a nickname chosen by a miffed, enforced adoptive father whose daughter had decided Cairo (the feline's real name) was no longer relevant.

The Lidl supermarket car park, on a retail park near the Algeciras ferry port, is another poorly kept secret among the French *en retraite* community, who gather there before departure to inexpensive winter warmth and respite for aching limbs. Small groups convened in and around their vans. Buddying up and planning for the trip ahead, we felt excluded and nervous. Registration plates, the first clue used by the itinerant motorhomer in foreign waters, indicated to us that there was only one other British motorhome parked there, and they weren't home. Facing the fear of our non-native tongue, we found a couple in conversation and blurted a crude *"excusez-moi, où sont les billets, s'il vous plaît?"* Our question was met with a small wince and a moment to absorb and translate our Nottingham-accented French. A blunt *"la bas"* response came, but the eyes and gestures said *"Over there? Surely you should know where to get tickets or don't bother going"*.

Reaching the little shop we joined the queue, it was only a few people long but still spilled outside. Once inside the door, shuffling forwards, we leaned casually towards the desk to hear what was being said in front of us, craning our necks to watch the process. We'd been travelling across France, Spain and Portugal, our egos were over-inflated by nothing more than managing to stay alive. We didn't like the feeling of fear from being first timers among the experienced. More truthfully, we had no idea whether we were about to find ourselves out of our depth.

When it came to our turn at the desk we could only think to ask vaguely for tickets to Morocco, as if there was only one way to get there. Juan Carlos, with a face closely resembling the sound of his name, smiled as he spoke to us in broken English. Squinting a little, we realised the English was mostly French and Spanish, and Juan was politely telling us he took only cash, not the bank cards we had in our hands. Only at the handy cash machine around the corner did we realise that despite having never met Juan before we'd left all of our documents with him - passports, driving licence and vehicle registration paper. As soon as the machine whirled out a stack of Euros, which we nervously split between us and pocketed, we hastily walked the two minutes back to our paper identities.

Grinning from ear to ear, we over-enthusiastically shook Juan's hand, as we exchanged our bank notes for a transparent wallet of tickets and customs paperwork before heading outside with our comedic, but appreciated, complimentary bottle of Spanish sidra, a type of cider, and a chocolate cake. A realisation and anxiety set in all at once. Months of fear and doubt would soon be tested, we were going to Africa, on the early morning ferry.

Our collective knowledge of Africa was sparse, gleaned largely from Bob Geldoff and his Live Aid appeals with images of starving, pot-bellied children covered in flies. With this as our main point of reference, our approach to stocking up at the nearby supermarket might be easier to explain. We bought big, very big. Pasta, rice, cereal, jars of sauces, chocolate, dried breads, fresh fruit, vegetables and meat toppled out of our already-full cupboards and our small, hard working fridge every time they were opened.

We'd read how tricky alcohol was to buy, and why wouldn't it be with around 99% of the population being Muslims, a faith that forbids any intoxicating substance. So, once Dave was full of food all remaining air gaps were filled with precious liquids. Small cans of beer disappeared under camping chairs, litre 'bricks' of boxed wine formed an inebriating wall on a shelf in our wardrobe. Then when it occurred to us that customs in

Morocco might not be too pleased if we attempted to smuggle half a supermarket alcohol aisle into their county, we hid it a bit better.

Dave's suspension groaned from the additional weight as our thoughts turned to a dilemma. The newest generation of Moroccans were supposed to attend school, however many of them preferred to carve out a career as adept beggars. Their number one request was for money, then sweets - *bonbons* or *caramelos,* as they're known locally. Wanting to be liked and accepted by the locals (and to prevent any damage being done to Dave) we bought a large bag of sweets, then a stack of coloured pencils and pads which we hoped would encourage them to go to school. The problem of which, if any, to place into outstretched grubby hands would be put off for later.

As Prepared as we could be, the alarm was set for 7am, an unheard of waking hour for us these days. It was a pointless act as our built-in nerve clocks popped us upright way before the tinny tune had chance to do its duty. Excited and nervous, the sound of a neighbour's engine starting had us peering alternately at the clock and our tickets. Juan had told us to arrive two hours before the departure time, but when we peered through the curtains, Lidl's bright yellow and blue logo bathed the car park revealing that many of the other motorhomes had already gone. Were we running late? The place was crammed full like sardines in a tin when we'd gone to bed, but now there were now just a handful left, curtains tightly drawn, either sleeping off a late ferry crossing, or like us eagerly awaiting the start of their adventure.

In the inky darkness, the early morning chill and heat of our breath misted up Dave's windscreen before we'd even left the retail park. His broken windscreen heater hadn't been a problem until now, as it wasn't needed on hot lazy mornings. Cursing in unison the windscreen misted as quickly as it could be wiped, as we trundled along the fast flowing roads leading to Algeciras port. Impatient rush hour traffic buzzed around us not helping our slightly frazzled nerves. Opening the side windows let in the cold morning air and our vision of the road improved as we shivered. But there was something magical in the air and not even the chill could dampen our spirits.

As we crossed the flyover into the port, the sun hovered just below the horizon, silhouetting Gibraltar rock. The sky around it glowed many shades of orange, pink and blue as the lights on the loading cranes twinkled. The industrial scene was a strangely beautiful sight, any urge to capture it on our camera remained subservient to the urge to clear the windscreen. The road had turned into a narrow strip of tarmac between rows of red and white concrete shepherding blocks which twisted and turned. Traffic was funnelled to its destination by unlit signs perched on the concrete blocks.

Our queue was mainly the familiar white cubes of European motorhomes, so it was a small number of Moroccan vans parked to one side that held our gaze. Men, dressed in floor length robes, their trainers and shoes peeking out from under the heavy, dark fabric, stood patiently alongside cars and vans with plastic sheets protecting a huge layer of who-knows-what piled onto the roof. The vans looked like they were sporting shower caps or huge afro haircuts, we wondered if we had actually packed enough stuff.

In front of us was a hurdle. A black Transit van, filled with, and surrounded by young Moroccans in dark puffa jackets, sat immobile in our path as the queue moved forwards. Britishness demanded we wait as the queue gap grew longer, and we grew more anxious. It must have only been a matter of minutes, which felt like hours, before one of the men saw our gaping, nervous faces and approached us. Surely he was a drug-smuggling queue troll, about to demand Euros for passage? Instead he smiled broadly and waved us through, then moved his van to one side.

At the ticket booth Juan's vouchers were smoothly exchanged for actual tickets which was a relief. Our research had thrown up a few people claiming touts tickets were no good for various reasons. We'd figured everyone used Juan so he must be OK; we were right and our weakling confidence took a tiny leap. Exiting Spain proved a simple affair. Charlie's EU Pet Passport, proof of his inoculation status, was proffered to the car-level window, far below any motorhome drivers reach. It was immediately returned; they had no interest in a small dog wanting to leave the country. There was similarly little interest in our passports too, a bored cursory glance from one official, a glance at the worn outside covers being enough to satisfy another.

Popping out the other side of paperwork alley, Gibraltar rock re-appeared. The sun had hauled itself over the horizon marking the new day and illuminating the mess of lorries, vans and cars on the quayside ahead. Stripes of parallel, clearly marked lanes for queuing existed, but were dismissively ignored. Groups of people stood chatting, animated with much arm flinging and hand gestures. Lorry drivers studiously ignored those gestures clearly directed at them as they slowly beeped their way through to the front. Our novice status was confirmed by our position in the pack, dead last. We even managed to get ourselves stuck behind a lorry-less trailer waiting to be moved.

The ferry arrived and slowly lowered its ramps like huge mechanical arms reaching out for land. Vehicles spewed out of its belly, eager to make land and complete their crossing back into Europe. Eventually the flood abated, followed by a long pause during which everyone stared unblinking at the official in a dirty fluorescent coat, who finally signalled to the mass it was time to board. The chaos organised itself through the necessity of a boarding ramp, and Dave finally bumped up the steep clanking metal, still dead last. Inside, an irate official edged us forwards to within, what felt like, millimetres of the vehicle in front, despite no one else waiting to board and a vast field of space behind.

Charlie's shiny food and water bowls were topped up, and his head overly kissed, before we dropped from Dave's door to find ourselves in a metal maze. The vehicles were so tightly packed in we had to shuffle, crablike, between them. Discovering that the next two vehicles were even closer together, so we couldn't fit through, meant alternative paths were sought by ducking under bike racks and wing mirrors to reach the stairs.

Juan's two hour buffer had seemed excessive, which on our quiet early ferry it was, a bit. But with no clue as to what bureaucratic hurdles we'd need to leap, and denied sleep by nerves, we'd obeyed it. Leaving the UK we'd been waved to one side for additional scrutiny, "*Any guns or knives on board?*" a bored looking customs official had asked, "*Erm, yes*", Julie replied, "*We've a drawer full of knives in our kitchen?*". Spanish customs had no interest in our knife drawer, so we found ourselves with a good half an hour to spare before sailing. We stood on deck watching last minute vehicles brave the ramps, explaining our wedged-in position. Behind us Gibraltar rock rose above the morning mist.

Still stationary, a mumbled multi-language announcement was lost to the morning breeze. If it was letting us know the restaurant had opened, it would be of no interest, a lesson learned on a previous crossing back home from France. A calm sea in port, inviting an oversized plate of sausage and bacon, can gleefully turn into a rolling churning cauldron at sea. No breakfast for us. Ginger tablets had been taken too, in a belt and braces attempt to stave off sea sickness. The announcement drew us back inside. A crowd gathering around the information desk assured us the lost information wasn't food-related. But neither of us could work out what would cause such a crowd on a ferry, other than the call to lifeboats, but we were still in dock.

Among the throng no English voices pricked our ears, but a second wander through revealed compatriots by what they held. In the hands of an elderly couple were the leatherette burgundy finish and shiny gold crest of two UK passports. They turned out to be less fretfully clueless, guessing that Moroccan immigration would check our paperwork and stamp passports while we were on board. The unruly mass of nationalities made it clear the official would be a busy man and we'd been tipped off that the Gibraltar Straits can reward sea-watchers with whales. With a choice between a scrum and the king of the ocean, we took to the deck, walking to the rear in order to watch Spain and Europe fade into the distance.

As the first of the mechanical arms released its grip, a lorry raced along the ferry terminal road. It turned and crossed the quayside just as the second ramp reached up into the sky. The driver jumped out of his cab gesticulating at the quayside staff who comically ignored him, carrying on with their business. He'd left it too late and reached for his mobile to no doubt apologise for literally missing the boat. As the ferry shuddered into life and we pulled away from the dock the driver pocketed his phone, and stood watching, helpless.

We slid slowly past huge cranes unloading cargo containers from hulking ships, before cranking up the speed as we exited the port. Soon distance made the cranes toy-like, and we entered the Strait proper, it became clear the notoriously choppy waters would be kind to us. Seasickness tablets were superfluous, although butterflies continued to flutter. Losing our cool, we headed quickly back to the immigration point, maybe the single official was an efficient paper stamper, had processed the lot and headed off for a cuppa? Maybe not. The scrum had now morphed into a line snaking across the ship. In it stood a cosmopolitan mix; grey haired, white faced couples, single dark haired, sun-tanned men wearing jeans and a jumper or a floor length robe, groups of men with very dark black faces in a uniform of jeans and thick jackets and one lone Asian guy who looked comfortable with his singularity. Making idle, nervous chat between ourselves we held a whispered conversation about whether to hand over Charlie's pet passport. Would it cause confusion as he wasn't here to be looked at? Decision made: we'd hold onto it unless someone demanded it.

Are all customs officers trained in aloofness on day one of officialdom college? It certainly seemed that way. Sitting on a low seat behind the information counter, our chap slotted neatly into stereotype, staring intently at a hidden laptop as he thrust out his hand for the next passport. Putting one aside, he flipped through all the pages of the other, presumably looking for evidence of some political sin or travel into enemy territory, before taking a mental picture of the photo. With a sternness that almost had us inappropriately smirking, he made lengthy eye contact before thump-thump stamping and snapping shut the passport. No mention of our canine stowaway below deck, we waited until we were a safe distance away before we ran our fingers over the stamp, reading the numbers we'd been allocated for entry.

A mandatory look around the on-board shop revealed a smaller version of those found on UK cross-channel ferries. Word must have only just got out that alcohol is hard to come by in Morocco as it was three deep around the spirits section. With the bureaucracy and window shopping over for a while, the lure of fresh air, open sea and wildlife drew us back outside. Positioned at sentinel posts either side of the ferry, an excited shout announced a fin had broken the surface, a precursor to a pod of pilot whales heading for Atlantic waters. A mother and baby passed right next to the ferry, our camera excitedly clicking.

Several more pods passed either side of us until our eyes were drawn to a small rowing boat crammed full of people being dwarfed by a huge container ship passing behind it. We were about halfway across the nine mile trip and the little boat looked so vulnerable and small this far out. Devoid of fish catching contraptions, any obvious explanation as to what they were doing was lost. Were they attempting to smuggle themselves, in plain daylight and through a major shipping lane, to Spain? We'd never know. But it did make us wonder what we would find in Morocco that's so bad people might take such extraordinary risks to escape?

Shaking off a sense of foreboding, attention turned to the coastline coming into view. Rolling hills, miniature houses, trees, cars and roads; it looked much the same as the Spanish coast we'd left, only with fewer commercial buildings. The port sat at the foot of the hills, neat, shiny, white and still new. Behind the docked ferries we could see a huge car park surrounded by a high metal fence. To its right insect diggers and trucks swarmed around, busy building Tangier Med II, the second deep water port which would include two new container terminals for cargo. The whole area was the visual embodiment of the investment being made to ease the transport of goods and people to Europe.

Another garbled announcement was interpreted through the actions of others as they headed below deck. Charlie woke to the sound of us unlocking the door. His bleary eyes, rapidly turning bright and playful, told us he'd happily slept to the hum of the diesel engines. Still shut in the moving car park the mass of motorhomes, cars and lorries jostled for position in what little space there was. Slowly the huge doors screeched their way open, letting in the daylight like another dawn, before the whole mess splurged out onto the quayside and sped off, like greyhounds from starting traps.

Dave lumbered down the ramp last. While the customs official on the quayside checked our passports, we anxiously watched to see where the other vehicles went. Signposting was minimal; the motorhome in front of us missed a turning and ended up at a dead end. We cheered as we made the turning, now we wouldn't be last to arrive at customs, a small victory.

Along the dock the fenced off area we had seen from the ferry was packed full of cars and transit vans. Matching the overloaded vans at the Algeciras docks, each had a huge afro-style bundle strapped to its roof, most of which were the same height as the car or van wearing them. Underneath, the cars and vans themselves were crammed full of either people or things; blankets, bedding, food, used toys seemingly rescued for a second African life, plus lumpy parcels of the unknown. If this was how much people imported, Dave was seriously light on passengers and goods.

The feeling of trepidation rose again as we reached the customs area. We'd heard tales of serious hassle from touts wanting to 'help' people enter Morocco for a small fee. Rule number one to avoid them was to look confident and act as if you knew what you were doing – which wouldn't be easy, we didn't have a clue. Even simply parking up we'd managed to be in the 'wrong' queue in the eyes of one of the port staff. Behind him his coworker had moved a barrier across our path so we couldn't go in the direction he was franticly waving us in, so we joined another queue of motorhomes in front of us, after all we'd all just got off the same ferry. He looked amazed and distraught, we hopefully ignored him.

Unsure of what to do next and wary of tout potential, we once again followed our fellow travellers example. At least one person from each motorhome was disembarking, clutching paperwork. Determined to make it into the country on our own, we grabbed all the papers we might possibly need; and both got out of the van; Charlie was once again assigned duty as protector. What to do next wasn't immediately clear, in fact, confusion reigned. Signposts in cryptic, curving Arabic reminded us where we were, but offered no help. Fortunately for us, if not the Moroccans, France had annexed Morocco as a *protectorate* for a good part of the twentieth century, therefore a cross-section of the population still spoke French. School-learned French threw us a timely lifeline.

In front of each queue of motorhomes lay a booth, behind it were more rows of booths, seemingly shut. Furtively searching for the infamous touts, we saw none - we were on our own. Approaching the open window of the booth for our lane the dark uniformed man within sat facing away from the small window. He glanced over and took our paperwork, stared at it for a moment and thrust it back. "*Attendez*", wait, he cryptically commanded. With this we obediently waited, wondering how this inaction might help us move forwards. Itching to avoid feeling and looking foolish, we took another chance with the booth; the sight of the same clueless European proved too much for its resident, who angrily slapped the window closed, threw open the booth door, and stomped off. Our faces creased, breaking the tension.

The first motorhomes off the ferry were now on their way. Each of them having spoken to an official outside of the booths before leaving. The short, round official smiling and joking with other motorhomers could be our ticket out of here. We waited cautiously for a suitable break in the conversation, to enable Jay to enquire, in his best French, as to what we needed to do. Delighted to be asked for his expertise, the peak-capped official smiled and happily explained the process, pointing to a distant unmarked booth we needed to attend to kick-start our entry.

Minutes later we stood amongst the dwindling lines of motorhomes, waiting for our names to be called so Dave could be searched. Beside us, overloaded Moroccan cars were being inspected. Customs officials curtly demanding loads be unloaded. We watched, incredulous as one man slowly and carefully unravelled a car height bundle wrapped in tarpaulin on the roof of his Transit. We didn't know if the officials were being this thorough with the motorhomes, as we'd been too captivated watching the cars.

By now we were the only Europeans left in our smiling official's area; he wandered over to us and asked our names. Searching through his pile of papers he found ours and asked which was our vehicle. We pointed to poor, lonely Dave, the only part of the queue left, with Charlie keeping guard sprawled out on the dashboard. This was it. The moment we'd been warned about. Customs officials rooting through your motorhome, taking your alcohol and anything else they fancied.

The smiling official glanced at Dave, looked at us and said "Anything special?", "Err, no" we both replied in a somewhat surprised harmony. With that he passed us a piece of paper, smiled, gave a little wave in the direction of where the cars were being emptied and wandered off towards them. We looked at each other, what did it mean? The exit was through the search area, or are we supposed to stop there and be searched? We climbed back into Dave, fired up the smoking diesel engine and crawled forwards. As we slowly made our way through the search area the expected raised voices, shouting us to come back, never materialised, so we carried on.

When we left the UK for a one year road trip, the idea of going to Africa simply never occurred to us. As a result hadn't bothered to question our insurers about whether they'd extend our policy to cover Morocco. Some insurers will provide a Green Card, ours declined; unhelpfully suggesting we use Google to find suitable insurance. We searched Google, it told us to buy third party cover at the border. The state-provided flimsy document would realistically only keep us from entering a Moroccan jail in the event we accidentally hurt someone. But as neither of us fancied a spell in African stir, we decided to buy it.

Still inside the freshly concreted customs compound, we parked up outside converted shipping containers that housed the banks and *assurance* office. At the tiny, grilled window, we leant forwards and explained we wanted to insure our *camping car*. The agent, dressed in an ageing white shirt, thought for a moment, then uttered in English, "*€260, 30 days*".

Was this a test? We knew €100 was the going rate. Doing his best to look shocked and angry, Jay issued a "*Quoi? Non, c'est trop cher?*" challenge; too expensive, come up with another number. This worked surprisingly well, prompting a long telephone call, in an unidentified language. We managed to pick out the odd mention of *caravan*, which reassured us he wasn't on the phone to his girlfriend but worried us that we were getting insurance for the wrong type of vehicle. Slamming the phone down he leaned forward a little so as not to be overheard "*€92, 30 days*". Sold and smug, we took the scrap of paper, confident of its potency due to the small hologram it bore.

Next door in the bank shipping container we changed our remaining Euros into Dirhams. We were given 10.9 Dirhams for each of our Euros, but in our minds we rounded it down to ten, making it easy to mentally work out what things cost. The odd currency resembled monopoly money, the same way Euros did when we first changed over to them a few months ago. We made sure to ask for some Dirham coins too as we'd been advised we'd need change for tips. As it turned out, we didn't get enough of the stuff.

We belted ourselves in and drove to the guard at the port exit for a final paperwork check, and confirmation as to what the smiling official's hand signal had actually meant. He waved us through, we'd done it. We were in Morocco, Africa. Out of earshot of the officials, driving on a smooth, wide strip of black, fresh tarmac, we both let out a huge whoop of delight. The mastering of the physical processes to get to this point wasn't, we realised, the source of our pride, more the fact we'd overcome a fear. We were in!

FINDING OUR WAY

Peering from the ferry we'd been surprised at the folds and ripples of the land, hardly a flat spot in sight. An artist would need a simple palette to capture it; ochre, a deep green, and a light grey for the strip of tarmac, which narrowed, climbed and aged with each kilometre. Before leaving Spain we'd bought the Morocco maps for our satnav, which was spit-glued to Dave's windscreen. Its green line, twisting bottom to top, signalled the route to take. It would get us where ever we needed to go, however, we'd long ago worked out not to fully trust the little box. Its silicon brain had nerves of steel which previously encouraged us up improbably steep and narrow streets, our wheels spinning on wet cobbles. Such escapades earned the surly, argumentative and stubborn madam the name of Shat-nav, and we were now defenceless against her decisions. Unable to find a road map of Morocco at Algeciras port or any of the supermarkets nearby we had nothing to use to argue against Shat-nav - we were at her mercy.

We drove in silence, absorbing the surroundings through Dave's wide windows. There wasn't a building to be seen anywhere, yet there were people along the side of the road; alone, in pairs or small groups. Some sat, or rather crouched, in the early morning sunshine, while others walked, heads covered with a scarf or the hood of a floor length dark robe. Several stood, gazing intently at us as we passed. Occasionally a hand would point along the road, up the slope we were crawling along. It was unnerving, we weren't used to being the centre of attention. Assuming the worst, we feared for our safety, not daring to slow down, let alone stop, worried that we would be overpowered and robbed. These people were clearly poor, their sun-dulled clothes announced it like a badge, some of them would be desperate.

A temporary road sign shook us from our thoughts. Arabic scroll along the top, underneath in French: *Police, Stop*. Even without the sign, the worn and crude metal stingers snaking across the road, forming a chicane, announced an obvious intent. On this slope, Dave didn't take much slowing and we halted at the sign, silently, nervously awaiting instruction from the three armed and uniformed policemen who stood relaxed, chatting and unaware of us. We itched to move, to reach for stowed passports, to be ready with the insurance paperwork but we didn't dare. An officer stepped away from his comrades, glanced at us and flicked his hand forwards, his stance self-assured, his mannerisms arrogant. We were confused, the quick twist of the hand was barely perceptible, was it an instruction? Glancing sideways at each other, Dave held his ground. Sensing hesitation the officer recognised our greenness. He bent his head slightly up the road and gave a second, more pronounced, but still effortless wave. We pulled forwards slowly, eyeing the threatening upright stinger spikes while smiling at the guard who stared back emotionless; he'd probably seen the likes of us a thousand times. Once we were through the check-point a mixture of elation and concern swept over us; things were very different here to Europe.

Occasionally respected and equally loathed Shat-nav presented us with a challenge; a steep drop down and right hand turn onto the road below, the intersection forming a wide V shape. We envisaged Dave beached by his overhang, all four wheels spinning and us sat above, captains of calamity. Both naive braveness and a mild desperation to not fail at the first hurdle urged us on. As we skipped over it, without a scrape, things were looking good, driving here was going to be fun. Almost immediately our optimism was curtailed, a small roundabout signalled what was really to come, as a middle-aged man nursed his tiny, wheezing motorbike around it the wrong way, waving apologies and smiling at our gaping faces. We burst into laughter.

Manicured grass verges and tall trimmed palm trees separated us from the beach and the Mediterranean. New apartment blocks lined the landward side, neat blue and white lamp posts marking out the beach promenade. We could have been back in Spain, but for the small clues telling us something was amiss. A group of sheep, half-watched by a young man in denims, chewed on a corner of the perfect grass verge. Further along scraggy, devilish goats chomped on the same unlikely pasture. In a dusty patch of land between buildings camels sat in the sunshine, our necks craning to see this extraordinary confirmation that we were in Africa.

Less obviously, something felt odd, misplaced or missing. The place had the hallmarks of our European upbringing, but with a hint of the fake about it, like it had been staged just for us. No-one sunbathed on the empty beach. The tarmac ended abruptly in sparse grass which ensnared migrating white litter. A metal trap bobbed along on car-wheels, drawn by a resigned horse, the hoody-wearing driver lost in a reverie. We were driving through an African replica of a European holiday resort.

The non-incident with the steeply dipped road convinced us to spend some of our Dirhams on a roadmap. Another strangely familiar, yet not quite the same, sight came into view; a petrol station, it's bright blue sign declaring it to be *Afriqua*. Pulling in, we bypassed the fuel pumps, our diesel tank was emptying but we had limited Dirhams and enough fuel for another day or so. Julie jumped out of Dave and nervously entered the shop - a typical occurrence in our *Jay drives, Julie does the other scary stuff*, unspoken agreement. Garages in Morocco, we were later to understand, form one of many places where men meet to drink mint tea and stare. As Julie passed, one of the two men drinking at the table and chairs set up outside, stood and followed her.

Brightly-lit shelves attempted to look full; their contents carefully pulled forward and spaced out. Looking around, two obvious things were missing from the picture - prices and maps. The man spoke an unknown language, Julie's confused face prompted him to try again; "*Bonjour?*" French worked, a few words of response were formed and from under a display box on one of the shelves a dusty, folded Michelin map appeared. The map was wiped and presented with a flourish and a request for 100Dh. Without thinking 100Dh was handed over, only later did we consider if haggling was the norm in petrol stations too.

Pulling open the door to Dave, the map entered first, held up in triumph. As the man went back to his drink, we took our time unfolding the map to find where we were, and to read off some of the names in bold; *Fez, Meknes, Rabat, Marrakech.* Splashes of brown diagonally across the paper were labelled with the names of elegant-sounding mountain ranges: *Rif, Moyen Atlas, Haut Atlas,* all in French, but we didn't care - we had a map.

The names of the cities meant little to us, our guidebooks were barely thumbed. The mountains worried us, either side of the road small triangles were labelled with heights: *2545m, 3192m.* The air was cold, snow on narrow mountain passes ranked high amongst our arsenal of fears. A couple of attempts to fold up the concertina map resulted in it suddenly gaining thickness; on the third attempt we worked it out. Flattening the map to show the section we were in we slowly pulled off, Julie tracking our progress with a green highlighter pen.

The road stretched itself wider into a dual carriageway which became harder to negotiate than single lanes in each direction. The rough, damaged outside lane had Dave shaking, cupboard contents complaining and threatening to reduce themselves to small pieces. Moving to the slightly smoother 'fast' lane we forced decrepit Mercedes taxis to undertake us, as they bounced past their rear windows were filled with innumerable faces, staring accusingly in our direction.

Reaching Martil, our refuge for the night, and a summer resort for the population of inland Tetouan, the campsite itself eluded us. After a couple of passes along the main road there was still no sign, in desperation we pleaded with Shat-nav to show us her 'points of interest'. She proudly displayed the campsite along with its address and directions to get there, great news for our immediate problem, but not so good for the rest of our trip as this was the only Moroccan campsite she knew of. As we navigated in the campsite's direction we spotted a very faded sign, half hanging from a lamp post, welcoming us in.

During our trip across Europe we mainly spent our nights free camping, parking up and sleeping in car parks or alongside a quiet road or beach. Our minimal research of Morocco had made it clear that we needed to stay on a campsite or in guarded parking (a car park where a high-visibility jacket qualified a man to collect cash from you in return for watching your vehicle). In Portugal and Spain a few old hands who'd visited Morocco over the years advised us *"it's not the same as it used to be, the new King's clamped down".* Meaning free camping was no longer the done thing. Another sage piece of advice offered was that Moroccan campsites aren't up to European standards. One bloke we'd spoken to simply told us "*They stink. Literally*". So we didn't have high expectations.

The campsite didn't look too bad, our opinions buoyed by its popularity, there was hardly a free space among the ranks of shining white French registered vehicles, many of which we recognised from our ferry crossing. Approaching the small shed/reception at the entrance, the occupant slid over two paper forms for registration. They requested our name, address, passport number, occupation, where we'd come from and where we were going - about the only things they didn't ask for were shoe size and inside leg measurement. We had a little difficulty on one section as we had no idea of our onward route, but we filled them in as well as we could. Some days later a French campsite owner told us that the details are used by the police to track down missing foreigners. Reaching the edges of our map in the days to come, we would start to understand why people could so easily become lost.

With Dave hooked-up to a foot-high, green metal mushroom, the electricity distribution point, Charlie demanded to stretch his legs. Leashed up, he sniffed around the site, meeting a few poodles and west highland terriers, while we took the dog walk as an opportunity to sneak a look inside the toilet blocks. Both sets of facilities were unsurprisingly similar, entry being met by the fluttering of birds in the open roof space. Pushing open an unmarked door presented a shower tray with a paint-peeled pipe above it, no shower head. Another unmarked door opened into a Turkish loo, stained deep brown. Unsurprisingly, in the time we spent on the site, no-one used these half-hearted facilities, except to empty a chemical toilet cassette or two.

With Charlie satisfied by whatever it is dogs need to know about their surroundings and us satisfied that Dave has his own shower and toilet, we left Dave safely tucked behind the walls enclosing the site and set off along the seafront towards the local town. The air was cool under an overcast sky and the few people on the sandy beach were more than fully clothed; women wore head scarves, many men wore a theatrical pointy-hooded floor-length robe, the djellaba, over their clothes. Charlie's delight for the sea, or more correctly its disgorged collection of expired seafood, had to be reigned in. We'd read that dogs and Islam don't mix; we knew that, but not much more.

A realisation struck us as we tried hard not to stare at the brown faces and unusual clothes, people were staring at us. Here we were the ethnic minority. It was a strange feeling, not a threatening one, just an uneasy one, something we weren't used to. We'd tried our best to blend in and respect their culture, we hoped. We'd been careful to ensure only our heads and hands were uncovered, but our light skin and the hint of ginger in Jay's beard gave the game away. There was also one small thing we hadn't considered which made us stand out. Outside of the confines of the campsite, no-one else had a dog. Sure there were big, scary, barking guard dogs and wild dogs around, but Charlie, the fluffy brown and white thing trotting along beside us on a lead, led to open stares, squealing sidesteps and fascinated prods from children as opposed to the cooing and stroking he'd received in Europe.

Our trip into town had a mission, connection to the internet. We kept an internet diary, a blog, which we updated every day while travelling. It served to re-assure our families of our well-being, and pushed us to squeeze as much as possible from our time away. With this world-wide sentinel watching us, we made sure not to loll around in comfortable beach resorts with cheap drinks and little learned. In order to keep up our blog we needed to get access to the internet, in Africa, it sounded impossible. Jay's love of technology meant he'd done his homework on this point and not only was it easily possible, but it was much cheaper than in Europe. All we had to do was find a shop of the Moroccan equivalent of Orange or T-Mobile, *Maroc Telecom* among the streets of Martil.

The first shop on the edge of town had the orange and blue logo we recognised from the company's website, another sign alongside proudly announced *teleboutique*. Walking inside, our eyes rolled around in the dark interior, walls stacked high with boxes of everything except phones. The near-emptiness we expected of a mobile phone shop was missing, this wasn't the place. A few words in French to the owner resulted in mutual confusion. More words, scrabbling around at the bottom of our barrel of French vocabulary, gained a thread of understanding. The shop keeper walked out and pointed further into the town, uttering a few more words, probably important, but lost on us.

Turning off the seafront the neatness and order of the soldierly lampposts collapsed. Within 20 meters grass turned to dust, tarmac crumbled and clear-glassed apartment blocks became shabby, lines of shops with solid metal doors like you would expect to see in a prison. People seemed to stream from side streets, most with a busyness to them, others sat holding a bag and stick, as if they were their last possessions. The European veneer was further stripped away as the trades spilled out onto the pavements and into the road.

A tyre cut in half stood along the red and white painted curbstones, next to it a car on wooden stands with a half an oily mechanic protruding from underneath. Weaved baskets competed for new owners with tartan canvas bags. Stacks of eggs in large trays, hundreds of them, had us wondering just how fresh any of them could be. Tiny shops, some branded with a hand-painted *Coca Cola* logo, were packed to bursting, often with a counter across the doorway; if you wanted to buy, you had to ask for it, no browsing, no taking your time. Vegetables climbed around our knees. Plastic buckets and dishcloths sat alongside hair dye, spices and tubs of black goo. With no other white faces in the crowd, we felt alone and elated, and glad we'd stocked up in Spain.

The Maroc Telecom shop was closed, a European style metal shutter pulled down over its single window. A letterbox sized gap enabled us to see in to ensure we'd found the right place. The opening hours, sellotaped to the door, confirmed that like its Mediterranean cousins across the water, the shop was on a long lunch break. Our minds spinning with the sights and smells, we headed back to Dave to wait for it to reopen. A dusty alleyway between plain concrete buildings promised a short cut to seafront safety; too afraid to walk down it we took the long way round.

Back on the seafront the low mid-winter sun had made an appearance, but was unable to lift the temperature. A group of men on the beach looked engrossed in a game of tug-of-war, as a few people stood around watching, we stopped too. Looking closer, the rope, that the two groups were pulling at each end of, was going into the sea. It wasn't a game at all, they were physically hauling in a fishing net. The amount of rope already on the beach made it clear that this had been going on for a while, and as heaving men dropped out they were replaced by others who had been resting. There were no clues as to how the net got out there, but as we watched the gap between the groups got smaller and the net and its contents came ashore. One man peeled off from the group to grab a couple of buckets into which fish were sorted. We'd only ever seen beaches being used for recreation, here they were a workplace. We hoped they got a good catch for all the effort and wondered how the catch would be shared out.

Back in our two-roomed home a siren erupted in the air above Dave, both of us instinctively checking for activity from our neighbours, nothing. No, not a siren, the shape of a voice appeared within it, half singing half wailing. The call to prayer, once made by men shouting from the heights of mosque minarets, now made its way into the ears of the believer via loudspeakers. One such minaret right next to the campsite, ensured we too heard the call, which takes place five times a day to remind Muslims of the key pillars of Islam and requesting their communication with Allah. We listened in silence to the soulful, timeless singer, absorbing the sound.

Flipping open the map, which filled our only table, we started to plan, cross-referencing known campsites with guide book promises. A couple of hours later the map had lost its plain virginity and was covered in sticky, brightly coloured arrows cryptically labelled with the source of the information: *RG* for Rough Guide, *LP* for Lonely Planet, *CCI* for Campingcar-infos.com, a French database of motorhome parking places. The mountain ranges marched straight through the forest of arrows, we frowned and headed off back to town, leaving Charlie to the peace of Dave.

The cash machine whirled out Dirhams, as we huddled close to it, splitting and hiding the notes, we joked that the wad would probably last us for our entire trip. The Maroc Telecom shop was now open for business, the shy young woman serving appeared older than her years in her headscarf. A box of tricks, not much bigger than a cigarette packet, containing a 3G dongle and SIM card, was all that we needed to wirelessly connect to the internet as much as we wanted during our month in the country. When it appeared from beneath the tiny counter we handed over 200 Dirhams, just under £20, a fraction of the price we'd pay for a similar item in Europe. That was it. No paperwork, no passports, no bank account details, no need for a Moroccan phone number, none of the things we'd expect to be asked for.

With another purchase under our belts our confidence had grown a little, feeling brave we set off to explore the town. The taxi rank outside the shop was a row of beige Mercedes, one of the two kinds of taxi we'd read about operating across Morocco. Bluntly titled *Grand* and *Petit,* we were looking at a rank of Grand taxis, pensionable Mercedes, which travel with an incredible six passengers, plus the driver. The Moroccan equivalent of the Intercity train, they haul people and luggage between towns, at a slower but certainly not leisurely pace. We didn't have any plans to use them, but if one of us did, losing all semblance of personal space, they'd either need five other passengers (preferably close friends), be prepared to pay for any empty seats or to stand about and wait for enough people going in the same direction.

The Petit taxis stood in an opposing row further up the street. The Fiat Panda sized cars, all painted the same shade of red, were fitted with rusting metal roof racks to carry luggage. They're punished for their scale by being banned from leaving town boundaries, but on the plus side we could get in one and leave, without waiting or cramming in with five strangers. Spotting both types of taxi, we self-congratulated ourselves, our limited research meant we knew at least some small facts about where we were.

Our walk around the town lasted long enough for us to be bustled down a couple of narrow alleyways lined with stalls selling fruit, round discs of bread and live chickens. With £200 worth of Dirhams shared between us and busy streets, nerves soon got the better of us, so we headed back to Dave before the sun started to set. That evening we remained half tense; the unknown of the next day looming. We also felt like celebrating; whatever was to come we'd gotten this far. Incongruously within the boundaries of the rather grubby campsite, an immaculate restaurant sat atop some steps. The menu posted outside sounded authentic; although we eyed up the low prices more than the mystic-sounding food. It also stated that you could take food back to your motorhome - what was the point in that? We soon found out.

Once sat down at a table inside we shivered, the lack of heating reminding us it was January. Two other couples were sat some distance from us, retired French, eating quietly and speaking fluently with the staff. They took their coats off having been prepared and dressed warmly, our coats stayed on. Our mint teas arrived, which we wrapped our hands around, a sweet green hot water bottle. It tasted delicious, our teeth immediately crumbling under the assault of at least five teaspoons of sugar. Julie could only manage one glass of the stuff, so was delighted to find Fanta Lemon had made it to Africa. Tagines of chicken and kefta arrived, they were the only items available on the menu. The kefta was a hopeful order, turning out to be seasoned meatballs layered with a cooked egg and soft vegetables. We devoured the lot of it, and a doubt started to tap us gently, this food is incredible, did we really need to buy half the beans and pasta in Spain? Nougat ice cream finished the meal and brought another happy smile to Julie's face. When it came to the time to pay, the staff had disappeared and by now our core body temperatures were dropping, and eyelids drooping. An investigation of the thankfully clean kitchen prompted a collection of our Dirhams. We practically skipped the few meters to Dave, plugged in our small electric heater, and fell asleep.

THE MEANING OF CULTURE SHOCK

The morning call to prayer hit Dave in waves, rattling around the inside, mesmerising us as we searched for the words in the song. It wasn't yet 6am, we turned over for more sleep. At 7am our tinny alarm clock, feeling slighted from the yesterday's redundancy, gleefully issued its urgent beeping. This second prompt, coupled with we've-an-exam-today butterflies, rolled us one after the other from Dave's drop-down bed.

We'd picked our next southerly destination the evening before: Chefchaouen in the Rif Mountains. Fellow travellers and friends Chris and Tina had crossed over into Morocco a couple of weeks before us and, having driven along the same route we were going to follow, they had sent us an email. They advised us to allow plenty of time, three hours of it, to make our way along a couple of innocuous-looking inches of red road. With no experience of Moroccan roads Shat-nav thought about it for less than a minute before announcing that it would take just over an hour to the chequered flag in Chefchaouen.

Leaving the site we caught a last glimpse of the sea glinting between buildings before it was gone. Any temptation to use Dave's ear-like rear view mirrors to see it again disappeared as the true nature of the Moroccan road arrived, from all directions. Stumpy Mitsubishi lorries, made as tall as they were long by tottering cargoes of hay, thundered along. Only a thin strip of windscreen left free of stickers and decorations for the hunched over figure within to navigate by. Three wheeled, covered tuk-tuks, Grand taxis, and donkey-drawn traps entered the mix. Whining motorbikes crawled along in the gutter, a battered tin-top helmet dangling from the handlebars.

Confidence and crawling seemed the most appropriate tactic for advancing through the melee. Ignoring the flashing headlights of an impatient lorry on the opposite end of a narrow bridge which we were already half way across: *I'm coming through, get out of the way*. Lorries ruled the roads here, or at least they did as far as we were concerned as they were about the only things bigger than us. It seemed if a vehicle stopped, it was assumed dead and swarmed around. We kept moving, slowly, hoping the European right-of way rules might, in some way, apply here too.

With relief we dropped onto an empty dual-carriageway, marked as a motorway on our map. With irritation, Shat-nav chirped her favourite phrase: *turn around where possible.* We'd accidentally made it onto the toll road, the one that she hadn't bothered to suggest we use yesterday, if only we'd had the foresight to buy a map earlier. We had read that the tolls here cost a pittance so we laughed off our detour, enjoying the calm of the empty road. Turning on the radio we were rewarded with the familiar crooning of Rod Stewart questioning if we wanted his body? No thanks Rod! He took the hint and was replaced with a French cookery programme; we listened intently but couldn't quite slice the dialogue into words.

The cooking lady accompanied us to the next junction. Getting off the toll road we paid our dues, drove around the roundabout and went back through the line of booths onto the toll road, now heading in the opposite direction; our movements closely followed by the bemused stares of the toll collectors. Reaching the correct road for Chefchaouen we advanced south, Chris' advice painting itself out in front of us. Oncoming lorries drunk on overloaded momentum had us sucking in breath, squinting and edging as far as we could to the right, Dave's tyres juddering along the edge of the tarmac. Little time was left for observing anything not directly in front of us, the dull red rocks and muted trees ignored. Small towns were crawled through as the road surface suffered under the heaving mass of market-goers. Gently pushing our way through throngs of people walking on the road, seemingly unaware of our existence, the uneven surface didn't really matter at this snail's pace.

A Grand taxi jerked to a halt in the dust in front of us, its dim brakes lights barely visible. Jay swung Dave to the left, narrowly avoiding a collision. As the new punter squeezed his way into the already full interior, we realised something: the many people we'd seen hanging around the side of the road were waiting for a Grand taxi with room for them. It was obvious in hindsight, they weren't modern day robed Dick Turpins, they just needed a ride. From this point on we looked more carefully at the faces along the roadside. Some appeared hopeful, catching our gaze and pointing up the road. Our lack of trust urged us on, with a feeling of guilt and confusion as we glanced around us at Dave's empty seats, enough for ten Moroccans and their luggage. Our yellowing middle-aged motorhome had never felt more like luxury.

The donkey to human ratio increased as we drove into the hills. If they were ridden it was mainly by men, and side saddle seemed the most comfortable position. Women only seemed to be able to ride on a donkey if a man walked in front of the beast. When towed along on tattered string, huge loads would threaten to collapse the donkey's skinny legs, although none stumbled. A kind of class hierarchy formed itself in our minds, based on the transport used: walking, cycling, riding a donkey, riding in a donkey cart, steering a small Chinese-built 100cc motorbike, taking a taxi, captaining a larger 400cc thumping motorbike and finally driving your own car. Driving a whacking great empty motorhome floated clearly above them all, we were rich as kings.

Dave's fuel gauge requested feeding. Another *Afriqua* appeared and as was becoming the norm, no prices were advertised. The boiler-suited attendant clarified the no-self-service rule by his appearance, and we handed over the keys *"plein, s'il vous plait"*, full up please. Black dials spun like 1970's fruit machines, and we worked out the price. At about a third of the price of fuel in the UK, Morocco would be a small place, at least as judged by our wallets. *"How does tipping work here?"* we silently asked each other with a look and shrug. Another driver handed something over. The attendant finished squeezing every last drop into the brimming tank, we paid with a wad of notes, and gave him a few coins in exchange for our keys. Watching carefully for a reaction, there was none, he pocketed the coins and stood to one side, looking up the road for the next thirsty motor.

Buoyant chat filled Dave as we pulled away. Rich by local standards we might be, but we still had a budget, and thankfully it looked like Morocco wasn't going to bite off too large a chunk. With a twist in the road we came back to earth with a bang, a sharp bang, which emanated from Dave's wing mirror as an oncoming lorry made gainful employment of our side of the road. The testing road only afforded a quick glance to confirm the mirror was still intact. Its completeness showed the lorry continuing on its way unperturbed. We uttered a few comments about our luck holding and pushed on, now aware that in Morocco it's no good simply watching only your side of the road.

Nerves still jangling from the lorry clipping it was less than a minute before a Jeep overtook us, nothing unusual as Dave's fastest pace wasn't quick enough for working taxis and locals, but then the Jeep's hazard warning lights flashed, and stopped. Again, a few more blinks, before the car pulled over into a rare area of flat ground to one side of the road. Assuming some problem from the lorry-kissing we pulled in too, cautious enough to park alongside the Jeep rather than blocked in behind it. The driver walked to our side window, Julie had drawn the short straw and opened it a little. *"Smokes?"* the man asked, smiling and miming with an invisible cigarette?

"Err, no. Sorry we don't smoke?" Julie replied, brain churning through possibilities and deciding he wanted to buy some cigarettes from us. He looked thoughtful, shrugged, and walked off. Only later, when an over-eager seller walked in front of Dave waving a small plastic bag containing a brown substance, did we realise we'd been flagged down by a drug dealer. He wanted to sell us cannabis or hashish, what's known as *kif* in the Rif Mountains, an area we'd clearly entered. Cigarettes of the tobacco kind were everywhere in Morocco, made more accessible by shops and stalls selling them individually. Clouds of blue-grey smoke lingering above cafés signalled that nearly every male smoked them, but at the local bargain price. No-one would want to buy them from a European.

At the outskirts of Chefchaouen we were waved through another police road-block, our fourth since we'd left the port. They were quickly becoming routine. Slowing or stopping Dave the officers would see his foreign registration plates and wave us straight through. Younger policemen might even smile at us, although this was rare. Local cars didn't have it so easy. They were pulled to one side, the occupant standing nervously, arms held still at their sides, as an officer sternly fingered through coloured paperwork.

Chefchaouen was a little way off the red road on our map, we needed to take a smaller yellow road with double chevrons on it. In reality, this meant a climbing test for Dave. He took the first gear scramble up a tarmac road in his stride before, at the last minute, swinging left onto a wide area of hard, ploughed dirt. The campsite entrance resembled a scrapyard, two wide blue metal gates, one of them half-swung open, were topped off with unwelcoming, although slightly decorative spikes.

Uncertain of the entrance procedure, as these vary between campsites everywhere, we pulled up to the gate. This prompted a thin, fleeting man to appear from a side door and fully open one of the gates. Behind him ten or so glinting white motorhomes were lined up to one side, parked on neat, level gravel, tall pines rising up behind them. Heartened by the sight of fellow Europeans, we reversed into place, our French neighbours were total strangers, yet felt like old friends from home.

Gate-man was also checking-in-supervisor-man. Standing under a framed photo of the current King of Morocco, King Mohammed VI he confidently named his price. We replied with an eager nod of confirmation before he gestured for the young girl sitting at an ageing wooden desk to present us with the information forms to complete. *"Pour aller au ville?"* we asked, wanting to know the best way into the old part of the town below. His reply went on a while, perhaps encouraged by our earnest nodding. In reality we only managed to grasp the odd word, but we got the picture: *the medina's over there, down the steps, ten minutes.*

Walking back across the gravel to Dave we took a detour to the other side of the site. Here the hill drops away and between gaps in the trees Chefchaouen can be viewed from above. From this vantage point only the newer, concrete block buildings were visible. Above them the bright blue sky appeared huge over a sweeping bowl of hills. Taller distant mountains greyed out the bottom part of the horizon, as the road out of the town to the south swept back and forth over the hillside between small misshaped green fields. Stood here in the camp we felt safe, the same iron blue gate which installed disquiet now installing trust. Charlie remained nonchalant, just another sniffing spot for him as he strained on his lead to sample someone's outdoor cooking.

Feeling a little giddy with excitement we decided to make acquaintance with our French neighbours, who mind-bendingly spoke with a broad Yorkshire accent. They were British ex-pats; the registration plates on their van had fooled us. Alan told us how the mismatch of passport to plate had also caused three hours of confusion at the border. His wife Brenda joined us when she'd finished preparing food inside their van and they both told us about their earlier walk into town. A young man had joined them explaining he was a student wanting to practise his English, he ended up giving them a tour of the town. Alan fetched out his camera and poked the buttons, we twisted about in the bright sunshine trying to make out the images of blue-washed buildings and robed figures on the screen among reflections of ourselves.

Our curiosity was piqued. We carefully stacked passports and money in our backpack and covered them to deter any pick-pocketing hands, before walking out from the safety of the campsite entrance gates. We'd read about guides in Morocco, often more accurately termed *faux guides*. In a land where many earn less than a single US dollar a day scratching at the stony earth, some tried to earn ten or twenty times that amount for three hours of regaling tourists. Who wouldn't?

Then a problem arose, too many got in on the act, often with little actual knowledge of their chosen haunt, and few words in a common language with which they could converse with their clients. The authorities chose to intervene and regulate, guides now had to prove knowledge and language skills, and were identified with a sort of back-stage pass in return. False, or *faux guides*, endure as the reward outweighs the risk of being caught and punished. Claiming to want to practice English and asking for maybe a small tip at the end of the act is a common trick. Brenda and Alan forewarned us, so at least we weren't about to fall for that one.

Our guide book had furnished us with a few Chefchaouen facts. A fortress was built in 1471 on the main trade route between Tetouan and Fez. It served as a base to stop the entrance and influences of the Portuguese from Ceuta, the enclave which today still remains out of reach of the Moroccans, only now in Spanish hands. More recently, and more interestingly to us, it told that any Christian found here before 1920, when the Spanish occupied it, was liable for the chop.

A few steps outside the campsite we find out why they are termed 'guarded' in reference and guide books. Gate-man, is also *le Guardien*, fending off those outside, ensuring peace for his well-paying flock of naïve wanderers within. Once outside his realm, we were fair game. A T-shirted young man wandered over, falling into step alongside us, mumbles something to Jay. "*Non, merci*", whatever he's offering we don't want. The rebuttal sails over him, unnoticed, and a string of names follow. He's selling cannabis, kif, chocolate, and a hundred other names for variations on a theme. "*La, shukran*", no thank you, Jay tentatively tries, one of the phrases we'd written out and stuck on Dave's bathroom door in a vain attempt to learn some of the local language, maybe Arabic will be more potent? The young man's face a picture of confusion and mock-serious offence: "*why are you here, if you don't want drugs?*". Walking on, ignoring him, he peels off, waiting for a real traveller.

A few more steps and the scene plays out again with another vendor, perhaps having seen his fellow tradesman fail, this guy was more resilient. His opening gambit, once again directed entirely at Jay, of a bright "*Bonjour!*" was met with an intentional stare of confusion from us. He tried again "*Guten Tag!*". We walked along, as he tried a gamut of languages, everything shy of Vietnamese, Jay shrugging at each. Our initial irritation turns to admiration, these guys were tough sellers, but in no way physically intimidating. We would have ended up with a bag of dope, but clung on to our 'we don't speak that language' game, until he slunk off, his face like his foe, a mask of confusion.

Free of kif floggers, the fifteen-a-side game of football on a flat area of dirt to our right immediately came alive, the ball forgotten mid-attack as half the team members leg it in our direction. Some are more adamant than others that we should hand over Dirhams or sweets. With difficulty, we smile, utter a "*non*" or two, and ignore them, the game gradually re-establishes itself as we reached the steps to the town.

Chefchaouen proper, the medina, is a bright mess of white, light blue and terracotta red. The jumbled buildings reached up to climb their way onto the hillside, held back by a long-redundant defensive wall. We stood and admired it, alongside a couple of young rust and white goats. Their wide-set eyes, under stumpy horns, took stock of us for a few seconds and they returned to chewing at thorny bushes. A boy on the football pitch saw us halt, and started in our direction; his pursuit pushed us over the edge and down the steps.

Each side of the steep, stepped path was lined with small pines and rocks. A robed, hooded figure here and there sat idly, watching us. Graves lay, seemingly where there owners had fallen, among the rocks, resembling painted concrete bathtubs sunk into the earth. The path levelled off and with a final kink turned under an archway in the outer defensive wall, leading us into what felt like a back door to the medina. We sucked in air and stepped through, with uncertain expectations. The medinas of the old imperial cities, famously Fez and Marrakech had fierce reputations as mazes, impossible to navigate, a blaze of activity and opportunities for the faux-guide. Alan had reassured us that Chefchaouen medina wasn't like that and was a benign place. We turned around and looked back at the doorway, memorising a few details to help our exit back into the open later.

The medina itself slopes up a hill. We turned left and walked uphill along the passageway closest to the defensive walls to get our bearings. We found ourselves alone, noises drifting up from below. The tight walls, washed with a warm blue, stretched up above us. Black tangled electricity cables drew themselves across this blank canvas, twisting in knots across the passage. Charlie investigated this new world with his nose, his face tucked into the curved fold between the stone floor and the azure walls. Steps lead off to the more narrow streets below, blue or white paint folding along them reminding us of a thin carpet. Wooden doors, recessed a little, stood with join-the dots lines of black or silver studs, standing out from their bright blue paint wash, a heavy metal knocker patiently hanging in wait.

The reason for the choice of blue wasn't clear; some sources indicating an unlikely defence against the hungry mosquito. Our own cynical interpretation of a tourist trap was trumped by a more realistic reason: a 500 year-old tradition, instigated by Jewish refugees from the unenlightened horrors of the Spanish Inquisition. They'd used the ubiquitous colour to remind them of the power of their god; a function fulfilled these days for another god by the enchanting call to prayer.

As the narrow alley curved around to the right, life appeared. The undersea blue becoming the backdrop for goods hanging on nails, or stacked carefully on the floor or wooden stools. Brown leather bags with long looping handles, deflated leather foot-stools their panels of colour filling the surface with a flower pattern, thick striped woollen blankets and children's coats. Intricately hammered round silver trays stood balanced on end alongside swan-necked genie-shaped teapots. A hanging string instrument caught our eyes as we compared the thin totem-pole patterned, fret-less fretboard and round hole-less sound box with our pet Ukulele packed safe in among clothes in Dave.

Many goods stood unguarded, no sign of a shop keeper, obvious potential for the unscrupulous? The visible owners sat on chairs in the alley, clothed in plain or rainbow coloured robes. Most simply watched us as we walked past, attempting nonchalance as we wondered whether this was an elaborate set, immaculate acting played out just for strangers? One shopkeeper calls to us and our heads look down, the floor becoming fascinating. He tries again, this time in English *"Come on, what are you nervous of?"*. He had a good point. Feeling a little shamed, one of us acknowledged him, turning and giving a smile and thumbs-up; returned by the keeper with a creased smile and shake of the head.

Around the corner, a robed man sat at his stall, a tiny wooden carriage, with a few sweets separated into different compartments in front of him. Jay's awkward enquiry in French confused the owner. Mime was called for, a small handful of sweets, carefully picked up with the right hand (traditionally the left is used for, ahem, personal hygiene) was held for the man to inspect. Looking confused the man named his price and a coin was handed over. Something seemed amiss, turning around we saw his next customer buying a single sweet, ah. A mental calculation had the sweets at roughly UK prices, they were either luxurious things, or the seller had pitched his inflated price perfectly.

Alan had told us that today was a holiday, which explained many of the closed doorways, but as if to defy his information, more shops started to spring open. The temptation to peek inside doorways was too great. An elderly man used a manual sewing machine, his foot rocking on a wooden pedal beneath the folds of silk-like bright material. Gatherings of vegetables sat pitifully alone, perhaps aware of the overflowing marketplace ranks of their French and Spanish counterparts.

Jeans and t-shirted children laughed along the alley, until they saw Charlie. A typical response being a sideways leap with a yelp, ideally to the safety of a protective arm of a downwards staring adult. Our canine, with generations of careful breeding, resembles a ginger and white patched toy bear. His floppy ears, wide brown eyes, furry feet and short snout had drawn admirers on our trip across Europe, an unknowing ice breaker. Here dogs are different. Islam, we knew, required prayers from clean followers and dogs were not considered clean, sometimes quite a fair assumption in Charlie's case. The first scattering nippers regrouped, a braver one making a few feints and finally a grab for Charlie's back legs, delighting his rear-guard friends. Our mutt turned around, seeking the source of his torment. We were caught out, torn between protecting our surrogate-child pet and wishing to blend in unnoticed, as we had all our previous lives. Another grab and we swung off the fence, shooing the boy back, setting an example with a friendly stroke. Some smaller children would take up the offer, tentatively touching his back, mouths open in fascination.

In quiet stretches between shops, we spoke in hushed, excited tones to each other, *"all these robes, it's surreal?"*, *"what about the guy with the sewing machine?"*. We were excited, wandering among this apparently ancient world, even an oncoming mini-van scraping between the walls failed to add a twenty-first century flavour. Our camera found itself angled along the ground and leaned against walls. Red-faced after being caught taking pictures of a breathless man, thunderously cracking a tree root with an iron bar and Thor-sized hammer, shots were, from then on, fired from the hip when we were unsure of etiquette.

The alley widened into open ground at the gate on the eastern side of the town, the Bab al-Ansar. Free of its walls, the road danced off, over a bridge and along the opposite bank of the nimble Ras el-Maa river. Bright carpets hung out airing on the high stone wall opposite, while below us a red-robed woman stood in a wide plastic tub, stomping up and down in Wellington boots, her head down observing the trampling. Another nugget of information from Alan was that clothes washing here was done by hand, or in this case foot, in the freezing cold water straight off the mountain. We were amazed to see this happening in the twenty-first century, just a few hours travel from Spain. Underneath two small open-sided buildings, more women and children rubbed material against the course ribs of sloping concrete basin sides. They worked with vigour, quietly chatting amongst themselves, heads wrapped in scarves. Wet clothes spread wide across leafless trees to dry, bringing them to life with a riot of colour. All at once, the scene appeared staged, a flickering TV documentary, but fitting, matching the sights and sounds we'd absorbed in our few minutes walk through the medina. The realism, we realised, was reinforced by the lack of tourists around, just us and one or two other more rugged-looking Westerners.

Looking towards the town we could see an outdoor tabled area with a great view over the river and of the clothes washing taking place. Men sat confidently at the tables, sipping at tall glasses of mint tea. They made no contact with the women below, a clear separation of duty, with no apparent challenge. Again it seemed a purely natural occurrence here, our understanding of present-day equality between sexes, or at least the struggle for it, didn't seem to fit. In amongst the wonder, entirely alien sights, sounds and landscapes, Morocco would do this to us time and again. An apparently innocuous scene would add a depth to hackneyed phrases we heard often without understanding. The small boy throwing stones, not in mischief but to dissuade a goat from wandering onto a road: *child labour*? The ever present staged portrait of the King, who retained power to override his government's law: *a dictatorship*? Our eyes were open, we looked and questioned, and tried to figure out a truth for ourselves. Back on Earth, we selfishly wondered about getting our stack of dirty laundry clothes washed, had Hotpoint made it out here?

Re-entering the medina, the downhill path bent its way into a large open cobbled square, the Plaza Uta el-Hammam, half-filled with wobbling chairs and elegantly-clothed tables belonging to a row of restaurants. A man slips into step beside us, "*mint tea? Follow me!*" Certain of us following he heads across to one of the restaurants. Pointing at a leashed Charlie, he nods his head, "*yes, yes, no problem*", and we take a seat, ushering the food-sniffing beast under a chair. Turning to catch a glance of drinkers behind us, all of them are drinking mint tea, glasses so packed with leaves they poked over the top. Our unease making us a little more observant than usual, we spot a note being passed to our tout from one of the waiters. We quickly check the menu for prices, but they were at less than half of the price of a drink in Spain (which we already considered cheap), we relaxed. Determined to take in the full experience, "*deux thé*" were ordered.

Our view was dominated by the Kasbah, an ancient mud-coloured castle which leaned out over the square. Arabic scroll ran around the top of a plain archway directly in front of us. Our scalding-hot drinks arrived and as we sat on royal purple cushions, the line of pointy-hooded elderly men opposite us, nursed their walking sticks. A man carrying a violin now occupied our view of the Kasbah. With an optimistic flourish of his bow he energetically created a violent racket of noise, helping us finish our drinks quickly, pay up and move along. Unsure whether he was actually a talented maestro we handed over one of our small stock of coins. It was a few pence to us but his profuse thanks had us thinking that maybe we overpaid him. We had much to learn, but it seemed the lessons came cheap.

Thankful of making a mental map and taking visual clues earlier, the medina exit was easy to find, above it the looming steps back up the hill. Blaming a combination of altitude (an unlikely culprit at around 1600m), a sugar rush, suspect water in the tea and exhilaration, Julie took to Dave's bed for the afternoon feeling wobbly, leaving Jay to once again unfold the map to plan.

Our insurance provided cover for 30 days, and Morocco was starting to look large. On our first trip, an overwhelming sense of self-preservation needed to be challenged, but we knew better than to tackle the Western Sahara. This massive expanse of land to the south west of the country, was represented on the map by a lack of ink. Eventually a single road runs along the coast all the way to Mauritania. To the east lies the Algerian border, closed to Moroccan traffic ever since this area of land was, arguably, illegally occupied in a search for valuable phosphorous. In our minds that area was the place for adventurous, fat-wheeled four by fours, green army fuel cans strapped to the side, not for us.

In fact, our spirit of adventure was being tested by something far more innocuous; little tiny black figures, bent in a speed crouch, skis pointing in various directions. "*Resort winter sports*" the key read, when unnecessarily consulted. Around Ifrane and Azrou, south of us in the Middle Atlas mountains, these minute silhouettes had us nervous. We imagined high mountain passes, sliced into vertical rock, ice and drifting snow being swept in our path. A worried email to Chris came back a few hours later: "*don't worry, the roads are clear, and there are snow gates to stop you getting into trouble*". Decision made, mountains, deserts, oases and gorges would make up our landscapes; Meknes, Fez and Marrakech providing the close ups of the people and their great cities. Rabat and Casablanca didn't even get a look-in, no-one we met had anything good to say of them, advice we'd usually consider ignoring, but our limited insurance provided a good excuse to avoid them.

Our evening leg stretch paused at the top of the steps to the town. Familiar constellations of stars above were hidden from us by the splatter of minor stars we never normally get to see. Below, the town glowed, an enthralling sight, a hubbub of voices, music, animals and cars as clear to the ear as the light to the eye. We'd stay another night, we decided, the promise of a market in town tomorrow and the need to mentally regroup. While supping a beer in Dave, curtains closed to hide our sin from Allah, we wrote an article for our website entitled *"we're freaking out, a bit"*. In retrospect, that was a little strong, but we now understood the meaning of the culture shock.

MARKET DAY

Eight in the morning and the sound of diesel engines thumping into life before crawling past has us awake and wondering. An early start, in the world of self-propelled travellers, heralded long hours of driving, as night time driving on the unlit, rough edged roads was only for the iron-willed or foolish. Pot holes, donkeys and people would remain unseen until too late. After investigating the campsite showers, we both used the one in the van. With the exception of a Dutch motorcyclist, who had little choice, no-one else used the facilities provided.

Late in the morning, we walked once more through the metal gates, Charlie in tow, enthusiastically hoovering the floor for scraps left unclaimed by the non-existent pet dogs here. Three paths lead away from the campsite; one to the left, one straight ahead to the steps, and the road to the right which we'd driven in on. The left path remained untried by us. Chris and Tina's footprints were there in the dust as they'd walked it a few days earlier. It led to a national park, and the final resting place of a donkey they'd seen, left to rot.

The road to the right, lined with white-spiked, man-sized cactus, brushed the new town. Paths of smoothly compacted dirt lead away from the road, through whitewashed concrete buildings, their glassless windows formed by cake cutters in a thinner square of wall. Unsure of the market's location, we followed a path downhill until it reached a junction. A head-to-toe striped figure walked past, hands in pockets, black shoes loping along, followed by a small white Suzuki van, topped off with an empty roof rack. More figures, all heading in the same direction, our human compass. As the path opened onto the road, the market arrived, with its many feet threatening to tread on Charlie's paws. Plastic boxes, used in our childhoods to move glass milk bottles on lumbering electric floats, were stacked with fruit and vegetables, ladies rotund even in robes bent over to inspect them. One vendor sat on his haunches, head wrapped in a light blue scarf, his neighbour used a cardboard-topped gas bottle for a chair, looking like a New York gangster fallen on hard times in his baseball cap and loose-laced trainers.

A shout from behind to clear the way for a donkey clomping slowly, laden with baskets heavy with blue sacks. The elderly lady leading the skinny beast had never heard of, nor would ever understand, the concept of a matching outfit, seven clashing colours working their way down, the result of necessity for warmth, ego unimportant.

Some figures appeared bored, some lost in thought, others smiled and joked. They all ignored us, apart from a goat-seller, leading along his varying-sized herd with bits of string, who smiled as Charlie investigated, sniffing from afar. We were getting used to the complete absence of prices, but other unusual things surprised us: a circle of live chickens held calm in one hand by their feet, worn and rusting tools splayed out on an orange blanket, battered metal weights and scales used to tally up vegetables and fruits. Butchering poultry in plain view, Julie turned away, the death of our food remains a taboo in the UK, but not here it seemed. We smiled at the donkey car park, a group of seven or eight animals unburdened for a while, restrained with a rope to the foreleg. The beasts appeared in good health, and no-one beat them or maltreated them while in our view.

Around a corner, underneath low sheets tied across the path to form a shaded corridor, smoke billowed and a familiar smell invaded our nostrils. Julie has a knack for sourcing chips, once finding a McDonald's restaurant from three streets away with purely a sniff or two. Drawing closer, the unimaginable appeared. Not just chips, but fried fish too. A much loved combination we'd not eaten for a fair few months. Food hygiene certificates are replaced in Morocco with portraits of the King. We hungrily took our chances and bought one huge round of bread filled with fried goodness between us. The cost of this meal for two was the same as Jay had paid for his handful of mint sweets yesterday, clearly something wasn't quite right with one of the transactions. Julie smiled as she tucked in, her face contorting seconds later as she discovered the ketchup lavishly applied by the seller was chilli sauce. This, coupled with the lack of batter and a full skeleton of bones, separated Moroccan fast food from that we were used to, but we still devoured it. An unfounded sense of achievement filled us as we sat on small plastic stools, among and ignored by the locals, trying to work out how much other punters were paying.

Too busy staring, dog shepherding and hip-shot camera clicking, we didn't notice the market thinning, as the entrance to the medina caught us by surprise. Avoiding eye contact rendered us unseen, no one approached us, we were slowly learning. Last night's internet research embarrassingly told us that we'd sat sipping mint tea right next to the town's famous Grand Mosque, positioned alongside the kasbah in the main square. Surviving since the 15th century seemed no mean feat in this country of mud-bricks.

The son of the town's founder, Ali Ben Rachid, had built it, and as with all mosques in Morocco, non-Muslims were not allowed to enter. No entry test would be needed for us, if there was such a thing, we were clearly not Muslim, so we made do with admiring the white and terracotta painted, hexagonal tower, wondering how we'd managed to miss it.

More shops were open today, testament to the truth of yesterday's holiday. In the medina's version of Saville Row, sewing machines, electrically powered if ancient-looking boxes, punched through thick materials. Around the craftsmen, the workshop walls were lined with finished goods. All bright colours, as though muted wear was banned. On shelves cut into the shadow comedy hats, typical of European ski resorts, adorned tatty, plastic mannequin heads.

Further along the narrow passageway things turned serious: brown and black robes, hallmarks of the mature. Since admiring gowned students celebrating term end in Coimbra, the ancient university town of Portugal, Julie had wanted a robe. The prices for the wafting black outfits in Portugal were exorbitant. Our mint tea waiter had advised us they were reasonable here, after one of us popped the unexpected question: *"how much for your robe"*? Haggling would obviously be called for. Haggling, is a dying sport in Europe, retained only for the purchase of houses and cars, and even then it is an edgy, distasteful thing to many, us included. We were frankly scared of haggling, and Julie was about to be initiated by the very best.

Walking past a few shops, their contents exactly along the lines of her desired wear, we slowed and Julie reached out to feel the quality of the cloth. An alerted spider, the shopkeeper, sporting one of his own garments, literally sprang from the door. With an uncanny eye, he initiated conversation in English: *"Come and look inside, many nice things!"*. Stepping in felt like walking into a wardrobe, not just because it was the same size, but because the walls were papered with stacks of folded cloth up to the high ceiling. Julie explained she wanted a black robe. *"For you?"*, the shop keeper questioned, with a head-to-toe glance. *"Yes, for me"*, she responded, hands clasped, attempting confidence. A superb example is held up, black-dyed wool: *"Perfect fit!"* the owner announces, no doubt about it, no need for a tape measure, the idea of a changing room laughable. Julie reached out and felt the cloth, pausing, dropping her head slightly to one side, a non-committal *"It's nice, how much?"*. *"220"* the man quickly announced, the game was afoot.

Julie had set herself a budget of 150 Dirhams. In anticipation of overwhelming haggling supremacy, only 150 Dirhams remained in her purse, the rest tucked into a jean's pocket. Another cloth feel and a scrunched up face from Ju, her turn *"too expensive"*. A surprise move followed; instead of a counter-offer the maestro simply asked *"how much you want to pay?"*. *"100"* Julie answered, and unperturbed the man reached around and picked up a similar robe, but flimsy, a thin synthetic material. *"Ah, no, I need a thick robe"*, Julie feigns shivering, folding her arms across her body and rubbing *"it's winter"*. With no response, Julie started to leave, only a couple of steps kicking the game back into life. *"180"*, a statement not a question, Julie paused, pretending to consider, *"130"*. *"170"*, and with another feigned exit, the deal was done *"OK, 150"*. The shopkeeper showed no emotion, no victory or loss. Taking the money and handing over the robe in a white plastic bag, Julie held it slightly aloft leaving the shop, smiling, feeling that the deal was a fair one. Trying the robe on in Dave, it turned out to be rather snug over other her clothes. No matter, it was always destined for life as a dressing gown.

That evening, we descended the steps for the last time, a torch picking out the path under the stars, its narrow beam careful not to find the graves on either side. Much of the medina was lit, the shadowed areas looked intimidating, perhaps hiding a villainous type, or maybe just a couple of the unending stream of kif dealers. One enterprising chap, having earlier failed to sell kif, or a tour of the small town, suggested a trip to marijuana fields. All the offers came to Jay we noticed, transactions were still expected to be handled by men here, something Julie felt quite smug about.

A restaurant not far from the doorway into the medina had been closed earlier, its menu translated into French and resting in a neat blue box. Finding the sturdy wooden doors swung open, we peered inside: before us stood a theatrical masterpiece. Blue and green tiles laid out on the floor formed a criss-cross pattern, one of a small number of schemes which seemed endlessly repeated as we travelled. Royal red carpets hid sections of tiles, above our heads the walls leaned inwards, red bricked archways, pinched at the top. Heavy chairs fashioned from an entire section of tree stood solemnly around small tables thick with white china plates and upended glasses. There was no animation, no customers we could see, no sound of a kitchen.

A waiter appeared, our minds recapturing old films about the Indian Raj with his dress and demeanour. Waving an arm to invite us in, he asked in

French which of the five tables we'd like. Choosing one, we shuffled our bodies into place in the tight corner, wary of sending the crockery flying in the silence. King Mohammed VI remained uninterested in us from his portrait vantage point on the wall to one side. Taking our order of tagines and soft drinks, the waiter left and we looked around, curious. Pushing at the adjacent wooden chair, it easily unbalanced itself, it wasn't made from solid tree trunk, but fibreglass or plastic. Tapped solid stone walls emitted a hollow response. We smiled at the clever fakes and again wondered whether the whole of Chefchaouen was a stage.

Our food, roasted lamb with apricots and a hunk of chicken topping a mound of cous-cous, was delicious, no trickery there. The price was expensive, by our tiny experience of Moroccan standards, but we happily paid it, not only for the experience but also the photos we sneakily took while the waiter was in the kitchen. Climbing the steps back up to the campsite, Julie became convinced a scrabbling noise heralded the waking dead, in reality an earlier-spotted turkey or goat was a more likely culprit.

THE MISSING CAMPSITE

Excitement and fear awoke us, as it would for the coming days. Using a thumb against our map we measured the drive from Martil to Chefchaouen. The 60 kilometres had left Jay with shooting shoulder pain and a strong desire to sink cold beer. Today's planned drive to Meknes, measured on the map in thumbs, was over 200 kilometres. Only one slab of beer hid among Dave's recesses, it might not be enough.

The length of our drives were dictated by the availability of campsites and guarded parking areas. While in Europe we'd focussed our research on ensuring we could get Charlie back into the EU and into the UK after visiting Africa. With legal documents read and a positive response received from the UK government agency DEFRA, we left the planning and discovery of campsite locations until we were in the country. The arrows on the map showed them to be distant from one another, explaining the early departure times of our neighbours; many of the spaces along the row stood empty by 8:30am.

The Rif Mountains, and their plague of likeable kif dealers, were soon behind us. The road straightened out and became edged by lush green fields. Fewer lorries barrelled towards us, yet the narrow road still called for pinpoint positioning as the shock wave of air whumphed into Dave as they passed. Dave's windows provided us with incredible scenes. Over-laden donkeys led in convoy by young women, groups of school-age children idle or playing alongside the road, modern-day shepherds convincing their goats to stay off the road seemingly by willpower alone. In places the sides of the road had been eaten away, like paper deliberately aged by burning its edges.

The town of Ouazzane provided relief. Big enough to have its own roundabout, we found an empty spot by the side of the road to pull in. Charlie had spent an hour or so accusingly observing us from his position of confined comfort on Dave's sofa. He needed out. Unsure of where we'd parked Julie stayed behind while Jay took Charlie for a walk around the dusty streets, ignoring stares, holding him still when a small girl reached out to stroke him, her mother nodding an approval and rewarding with a smile.

Within Dave things had taken a sinister turn. A young man had positioned himself a little way from the front window, staring intently at Julie within. Feeling his eyes, Julie stopped refilling water bottles and carefully moved our luxuries out of sight; camera, passports and the like. On Jay's return the lad remained motionless, staring into Dave. This didn't feel good, our confidence slipped, so we started the engine. The lad chose this moment to act, walking deliberately to the driver's window, without speaking his hand mimed the universal 'I'm hungry' sign, feeding himself air.

With a realisation we weren't being sold drugs or begged for money, we felt an overwhelming sense of charity. Unfortunately we also went into a flap, the wrapper-less, healthy fruit in our cupboard forgotten and a chocolate bar handed over. He took it, half smiled and stood back, allowing us to drive away, relieved, and thoughtful. Scruffy, sometimes dirty, with worn clothes, many people appeared poor, but none appeared starving, desperate for food. One of the pillars of Islam requires Muslims to give to those in need; as far as we could tell this indoctrinated charity system worked, but maybe not for this man.

Back on the open road, our status as relatively rich westerners was widely advertised through our chosen chariot. Dave is ageing, his outer body a faded cream colour. In Europe he appeared on the verge of failing, here he attracted near constant attention, as a possible lift, someone to sell something to, or just someone to wave at. People engaged in back-breaking labour some way off in the fields would sometimes stop working to wave; we waved back and smiled.

Passing a donkey cart loaded with a wide blue barrel we noticed the people going along the roadside in one direction carried huge, but light, plastic containers, those walking in the opposite direction were weighed down, bent over as they struggled with similar loads. Driving past their destination we saw the reason: a water fountain. We imagined running water had made it to almost everywhere in the world, how naïve were we?

Hidden in Dave there's a 100 litre oblong box for fresh water, an electric pump means we have running water on tap, even in our rolling home. These people walked miles to collect it, which defied belief, especially when sitting next to the water fountain was a white van, its owner using the precious water source to clean the dust off it. The contrast was extraordinary. A man washing his van, splashing water around in the dirt, alongside those without the most basic of services in their homes. No-one acknowledged this variance, it was simply accepted, some were poor, some were rich. We, of course, sat in the latter pool, but the sight had given us more food for thought. The image of the van shining next to people gathering water by hand fills our thoughts today, closed eyes bring it clearly into view.

Our long drive meant sacrifices. The Roman ruins at Volubilis were driven past. The remains were said to be well preserved, despite a crusading Moulay Idriss I sending his lackeys in a thousand or so years back, to help themselves to the nice bits. It beats quarrying and carving it yourself, and there were presumably few tourists about in those days to complain? We'd maybe see a few of the pilfered parts anyway, as we carried on to Moulay Idriss, the town named after its founder, just a few kilometres down the rumbling road.

Flinging itself into the air as we rounded a bend, the whitewashed and ochre square blocks of Moulay Idriss jostled for position on a single hill. The road went into an overdrive of perfection, a white on blue arrow advising of an upcoming roundabout, race track red-white kerb stones delineating the edge of the smooth surface. As Dave climbed the lower part of the hill, a small tangle of traffic had us confused, until a stick-waving policeman saw us and pointed up the hill. Further up we pulled into an area of land squatted by vans, brightened by hand painted orange and white speed stripes. As Dave's handbrake ratcheted into place, a face appears at the window. We shall refer to this character as *Arthur Daley*, for those who don't know the name, it's a fictional character from a British TV show called Minder, essentially well meaning, but a shifty, untrustworthy old chap. The comparison was initially based entirely appearance; as body belonging to the face at the window sported a fur collared, tan camel-skin jacket, similar attire to the small time criminal of the small screen.

Arthur informs us he is *le Guardien* for the car park and, since we're parked over two spaces (we scan the dirt for lines) the charge was double. Cue the fool: Jay whips out a wallet of Dirhams to pay for the parking, Arthur's eyes pop out and coolly pop back in. As we lock Dave's door Arthur enquires if we need a guide. *"Non, merci"* leaves Jay's mouths, travels through the air, transforms and enters Arthur's shell-like as *"Oui, merci"*. He latches on, chatting about the town, using some kind of trickery to actually lead us away from the town. Neither of us can remember how he did it, we walked on bemused. Attempting to ignore him had no affect, so we decided to play along. Cue the fool II: neither of us negotiated a price with this faux guide.

The tour took in mainly the back alleys as Arthur, we suspected, avoided the authorities and licensed guides. His ploy was not entirely successful. We stood back as two men threw a few accusing statements his way outside the main entrance to the mosque, being in Arabic, their content escaped us, but the intent seemed fairly clear *"Arthur, you chancer, stop nicking our business"*. Arthur explained in French, as he didn't speak more than a few words of English, that they were friends, before he showed us down a side alley where he went all peculiar. He insisted that standing on a lump of concrete would give us a view through a tiny window into the forbidden inside area of the mosque. We weren't really all that bothered about spying on people, so Arthur took our camera and snapped away for us. Later review of his photography skills showed intricate blue, red and green pattern work on the entrance, at various jaunty angles.

Walking around Arthur tells us the town is considered holy, being the place where Moulay Idriss I arrived in 789, carrying with him the new religion of Islam. One town not being enough, he kicked off a dynasty, including getting started on Fes. Being such a sacred destination, six pilgrimages to Moulay Idriss, during the annual festival honouring the saint, is equivalent to one Haj to Mecca. We've no idea of the truthfulness of this, but we did recollect that one of the pillars of Islam is the requirement to visit Mecca at least once in your life. It seems someone has done some ecclesiastic maths and, if we were Muslims, we'd each be a sixth of the way to Mecca.

The highlight of the tour had to be the *big panorama*. Arthur took us to a locked blue door, insisting it was his house. He pointed to a nearby cat saying it was his too, the cats reaction told otherwise, wandering off as he bent down to stroke it. It was clear from this vantage point that the town sat atop two hills, the one we were on and the one whose rooftops played out below us. Arthur again took our camera, snapping shots of us against the green-roofed mosque, our eyes questioning nervously *"how much are these photos going to cost us?"*. Pointing into the distance Arthur points out Volubilis, or at least the fog-covered area where the tiny stones should be. Eventually, to appease his gesturing, we tell him we can see it and he triumphantly moves on.

An hour and a half after we left, we're back at Dave's door. We're all drenched as it started to rain fifteen minutes earlier, but Arthur insisted on finishing the tour. No price has been mentioned and we'd spent the entire thing wondering and whispering about it. With rain running down our faces Arthur announces his price, it's three times more than we were willing to pay. As we edge towards Dave's door the exchange stays friendly, we tell

41

him we didn't ask for a tour, he tells us he's wet, we tell him we're wet too and we don't have that much money. Five minutes play out, and with all parties knowing it's an obvious mis-truth, but we claim we'll look in Dave for more money. Julie jumps in, acting skills learned rapidly by necessity, cupboards opened and theatrically shut. Outside Arthur starts to get edgy and impatient, for the first time we sense this could get nasty. Perhaps a final ploy, he quietly asks if we have any wine. *"Sure"* we answer, showing him a litre carton of the cheap Carrefour discount wine we stocked up with before we left. *"Give me two boxes"* he replies. Two bricks of red are rapidly rooted out, Arthur's demeanour reverting to the friendly person we initially met, requesting they go in an opaque plastic bag before taking them. *"How much did you pay?"*, he asks, mystifying us. When we tell him, he buys two further boxes from us, using the money we'd paid him for the parking, before disappearing behind the other vans. Eager to avoid any further confrontation we also left. Laughing about it as we drove towards Meknes, every mistake we could have made, we'd made; a compact learning experience!

The guidebook tells us that the only campsite in Meknes is within walking distance of the city centre which contains dramatic royal stables, a bustling medina, ancient mosques, intriguing dungeons and the Moulay Ismael Mausoleum, which us non-Muslims could visit. Only it isn't. The campsite at Meknes is closed. A friendly French man imparts this fact as we're parked up next to his motorhome in McDonald's car park, a safe haven sought, from the usual lively chaos of the roads, when our search for the campsite proved fruitless. Fetching his big French campsite book, he pointed at a site in Fes he'd had a recommendation for. Snapping the details on our camera, we thanked him, perhaps once too many times, revealing our relief. A section of motorway joins Meknes and Fes. Fifty minutes and a not-worth-mentioning toll charge later, we found the site just off the ghostly-empty motorway. Not needing to drive through the city of Fes, our only obstacles were easily ignorable waving from moped riders skimming along both sides of Dave in the rain. Campsites pay them a commission to entice you to their door, so they risk being crushed by a motorhome for the few Dirhams they would make. Clearly our discomfort in these encounters was a coin flip away from the desperation to make a living, to feed families.

Our relief of making it to the campsite dissipated slightly with the sight of a dripping wet electricity socket through which Dave was tentatively rejoined with the Moroccan grid. Batteries recharging, and the stack of Spanish omelettes cooling in the fridge, Charlie decided it was time to chill, his tour of Moulay Idriss had more than satisfied any desire to walk for the day.

Paws-planted in an anchor, he needed a bodily lift to extract him from Dave to accompany Jay on an exploration of the campsite.

While cooking, Julie answered a knock at Dave's door which revealed our French saviour from earlier, Claude. Language barrier awkwardly in place, Claude's patience is boundless. He's arranging a group tour of Fes, would we like to go? Getting the gist of the conversation Julie agrees, it'll mean Charlie spending a large part of the day alone, but he'll be fine. Later that evening, thankfully when Jay had returned, Claude pops by with the details. The cost is laughably low by European standards (and half the price we'd been previously quoted) for a full day tour with taxi transfers. We're excited; having company will be a bonus. Claude's hand was once again shaken vigorously, he was a great man to meet, and his easy smile was catching.

THE MEDINA MAZE

A couple of hours before we were due to meet our guide, Charlie and Jay exited the campsite on a 'tire the mutt out' mission. A snaking watercourse ran through nearby woods, mallards swimming on it reminders of home. They stumble across a sprawling building site, its sign, needed to aid the imagination, displays a gleaming group of white buildings on a grid of smart streets. Only the outline of the streets exist, tents to one side make up the rough winter accommodation for some of the labourers. Gravel roads awaiting black-top lead to a rise, on which the city below appears. At least the outskirts do, it's miles away and clearly a sprawl on a much grander scale to the one it's viewed from.

As they returned to the campsite, a fellow Brit asked Jay if he has any change. Apologising that our supply of small notes and coins is already depleted, the man tells Jay how his trip into Fes the previous day ended with the purchase of six small boxes of spices, for a large sum that he clearly had not wanted to part with. No haggling had taken place, and it seemed the vendor had, perhaps, won the battle by too wide a margin. Not content with the victory, the vendor was chasing him, by means of his tour guide, for the remainder of the money as he'd failed to have enough cash on him. We felt forewarned; Fes would have to work hard to extract more than a fair price from us, so we thought.

Our unreasonable dog guilt mollified by the deployment of a number of hidden dog treats, we left the van to the sound of an excited pooch scrabbling around. Waiting at the hollow reception building, no staff around, we attempted French on an elderly couple, asking if they were waiting for a guide. Failing to establish a common understanding, we waited close by. Shortly Claude arrived, his wife holding hands with his two boys, smartly dressed and well behaved. The thought struck us that while we were nervous of hauling ourselves around this African country, these guys of about our age were doing the same with children. Asking them about what it was like travelling with this extra responsibility, a raised eyebrow and a shrug told us all we needed to know: *"it's no different to travelling in France?".* Claude greeted the French couple, and our little group was complete just as a clean white minibus cautiously drove along the bumpy road into the camp. Our smiling guide climbed out, looking the part with a friendly face, short cropped grey hair and a brown djellaba. Announcing himself as Mohammed, he asked around to establish which of his six languages he'd be brushing off for the day. It was clear that the day would be predominantly French, and once he'd proudly shown off his worn and faded official guide badge, and tucked it back under his robe, he confidently ushered us into the van.

The fifteen minute drive into Fes was a relief. We relaxed back into the rear seat of the minibus as the driver negotiated the thickening, intermingling traffic along line-less roads. Our only strain, the translation effort, our poor French struggled at times with the string of information Mohammed imparted from the front seat. The flow would be interrupted from time to time with a shouted question: *"English, you understand?"*. Overcoming our English reluctance to inconvenience, we'd tell him no, and a précis version would come our way. The words were spoken kindly but scripted and dry, repeated a thousand times. *"The second largest city in Morocco, the most exciting of the four Imperial Cities as well as the cultural and spiritual capital of Morocco. With around 1 million inhabitants it's built on a grand scale, with surrounding walls that extend for nearly 10 miles."* He then went on to explain that *"Fes is really three cities in one. The core being Fes el Bali, the medieval walled city where around half the population live and we'll find mosques, medersas and fondouks, combined with a mile-long labyrinth of souks."* Mosques, we understand, the private and inaccessible Muslim places of worship, and *souks* we know, the thriving, pulsing and colourful markets. *Medersas* and *fondouks* escape us.

Mohammed continued: *"Next is Fes el Jedid, known as the new city but in reality was built in the late 13th Century and is home to the Mellah, the old Jewish quarter."* Finally as with most other cities in Morocco, we're told there is *Ville Nouvelle*, the newest part of the city created by the French during the Protectorate. The words are flat, no clue given as to whether Mohammed has any feelings towards the French who, like other contemporary European powers, were hungry for colonies. They effectively invaded, encouraging thousands of their citizens to move to Morocco and steer the country.

The route took us through Ville Nouvelle, a hybrid of European square and glass architecture, covered with a forty-year film of Morocco, streets gradually growing tattier. The driver pulls over and Mohammed climbs out with us, pointing to a tile and mud archway, to one side a square tower topped with pyramid-hatted crenelations: the entrance to the Jewish quarter. Over the road, we're stood in a wide flat area in front of a monumental archway, flanked by four others, the King's Palace. Couples took it in turns to photograph one another stood small in the doorway, two policemen stood brooding to one side. Mohammed's narrative continued, again without feeling or judgement: there's a similar opulent walled compound in each city, built when Morocco would trade goods with Italy on a pound for pound weight basis. Morocco received fifty pounds of marble to build the palace, in return Italian merchants happily accepted fifty pounds of oranges or hashish.

A shout from the policemen spun us around. Not looking at us, they were walking towards a tourist holding a camera near a smaller side gate, gesturing for him to come back to the main palace façade. Imagining perhaps an ill-conceived daylight attempt at robbery, we question Mohammed, *"No, they don't want him over there, that gate is a shit gate, does not look good for the King".* We all smiled and took another look at the wooden gate, which did indeed stand pale against the shining five in front of us, layered with golden metal embroidery, playing out familiar patterns. We wondered about this King, effectively a rich dictator, steering his country through a minefield of opposing extremism and social reforms. Mohammed smiled and said nothing.

Our next stop delivers us high up, another *Big Panorama*, only this time, unlike our tour of Moulay Idriss with Arthur Daley, there were no claims of owning nearby homes or cats. Our view from the sky was the strategic position of the white fort standing next, the entire city seemingly throws itself together into a rough sea of roofs, minarets and walls below. The dull new town stands further away, of no interest to the tourist; the old town is what we've come to see, despite not really knowing why we'd come. As with any grand-scale masterpiece of man or nature, spotting the fine detail, which makes up the whole, is elusive. No matter how hard we stare, individual buildings disappear like a baked bean in a jigsaw puzzle. The vast array of round disks pointing up to sky born satellites gave the scene a conflicting dimension; space-age technology was clearly accepted and embraced, reflecting our experience with Moroccan high-speed mobile internet. Copious photographs would later rebuild the scene for us, but the feelings of awe and get-me-closer curiosity were a one-off event. Mohammed pointed towards the green roofs *"there are over 160 mosques in*

Fes"; we wondered whether their respective minarets would call out for prayers in unison.

With growing anticipation the minibus crawls back into the city, jostling for valuable road space, making little progress. As the monologue halts, the mood in the bus is light. *"English, what you call this bouchon?"* French night-classes had taught us *bouchon* is literally French for cork, an apt name for the scrum we sat in. *"We call this a traffic jam"*, draws smiles and laughter as Mohammed translates.

Mohammed decides to move onto his next block of information as the roadworks constriction ends, in our seats we listen intently, attempting to memorise. *"There are five places in every part of the city"*. These it transpired were: Number One: A fountain for drinking water, although many of these have been dismantled as people now have water in their homes. Number Two: A Hamman, hot water/washing area for men in the morning and evening and women in the afternoon, we're told how that many Moroccans only wash once a week, on Friday before going to the Mosque. Number Three: A Mosque, it's purpose deemed obvious with no additional information yielded. Number Four: A Souk, covered shopping area. Number Five: A Fonduk, stables with accommodation above for travelling people.

As the minibus drew itself up into the city, we took a chance to unburden some curiosity and question Mohammed. *"What are these, Mohammed?"*, we point at a wall with a horizontal grid of numbered squares drawn on it, each square containing a different silhouette in brown paint, one is a bird, another a lit gas lamp, an olive branch and so on. *"They're for voting, an election."* He went on to explain, many Moroccans cannot read, but they can all associate a familiar object with a particular person or their political party, enough to cast a vote. The parliament has power, but the King retains the ultimate ability to make or break law.

We stop at Bab Bou Jeloud, the main gate into Fes el Bali. As Mohammed talks we stare through it, past the boiler-suited men pushing metal carts full of white sacks. The shape of the entrance is familiar, the pinched horseshoe carried high by straight, square columns below. A smaller scaled arch stands guard to either side of the main entrance, presumably for people although the stream of human traffic all uses the main gate. The wall the gate is in stands tall, doubling the size above the gate, blue patterns dance around two false windows. We're entranced, and eager to get into the labyrinth inside.

Unlike his European tour guide counterparts, Mohammed didn't walk with one arm high poking up an umbrella, flower, baseball cap or such like to announce his location. Instead he immediately blends in. There are 9000 narrow streets, laid out with no plan, even the maps of the place are vague and sketchy. We stuck close to Mohammed, not an easy task when the world has just stretched and with a ping, flipped itself over, spinning you backwards into a film set of yesteryear. In every direction something fascinating, a hand drawn sign denying donkeys entrance to a side street, piles of fruit and smoking ovens. Sunlight stemmed by overhead lattices lit ranks of mug-sized coloured cotton reels, hanging shirts, robes, sacks and stacks of shining dates. A skinned half-body of an animal retained its curving tail as it hung on a metal hook beside a hacksaw. Feathered chickens restrained with string stood on wire boxes, alongside featherless carcasses and piles of eggs, an almost poetic display of life stages. A machine behind them was being fed minutes-dead chickens, plucking away their feathers as still-visible feet twitched in the afterlife. A trader sat next to his only goods, four camel feet, lifting one up for closer inspection as we instinctively took photographs.

Mohammed's brown robe halted ahead of us. Pointing upwards he tells us this is the water clock, a series of windows and protruding wooden battens. Little more information is forthcoming; we later found it was once able to render the time using sploshing water and rolling balls. No-one has managed to prove how it worked. We're a little dubious it ever did.

Halting again a little further along we catch up with Mohammed and huddle around as he explains, smiling proudly, that we are at Bou Inania, a *medersa*, a theology college. As it was founded around AD 1350, it stood as the world's first university, centuries would pass before young upstartd Oxford and Cambridge would stand glorious in England. As both a place of education and worship, it is the only medersa in Fes with a minaret, and luckily for us, non-Muslims are allowed inside, with the passing of a coin. Past the decaying doorway, a square of azure sky opens above, the four pale walls of the courtyard around us devoid of a single inch of undecorated space. The decoration here was stucco, hand-carved plaster, only some hip-height sections of wall were clothed in protective ceramic tile. Surrounding the courtyard were small recessed plain cells, once used by students, now empty and barren. As we stood staring at the intricate decoration a man walked past to a screen across the far wall, washed himself and knelt down to pray, we averted our camera and discretely left him alone with his God.

Outside again, Mohammed walked us through more of the dramatic souks, Claude's tired children taking to arms and shoulders, as the pace was too much for them. Mohammed explained how medina is the world's largest car-free urban area and because it's closed to motorized traffic, donkeys, mules and carts are used to ferry goods around. These wide loads, taking the entire width of many passages, have the right of way, we must listen for them. We stayed alert for a few moments and then relaxed, until a cry of *'Attention!* a few minutes later had us pressed flat to a wall as a rough-haired donkey deftly hauled a stack of gas bottles past on an unpainted metal frame. Another donkey stood stationary, staring ahead, as used cola bottles were rattled into branded plastic trays either side of it. We stood enthralled at a sight the drinks company's well paid brand managers might have palpitations over.

A *riad*, literally a big house, plucks us from the dust, cries and bumps of the street, and slides us sideways into tranquil, green and white peace. Wondering what magic is used to soak up the outside noise, we look upwards inside a tight, two storey courtyard. Its base, forested with green plants and trees, hides a small central fountain and behind us a scrolled twisted metal stairway wobbles slightly as we climb it to a balcony viewpoint. Inside the riad rooms were are luxurious, reminiscent of redundant English stately homes, only there are no red corded ropes, the rooms are real, their purpose practical, a hotel oasis amongst the madness of the old city. The riad reflects age-old economic divisions, the haves stay here, the have nots stay outside.

The official tour guides supplement their wages with commissions from the various shops they take their captive audience to visit. Mohammed walked a fine line for us, we suspect Claude's diplomacy may have been at play. We visited many craft shops, all of which were workshops where the goods were not only sold but also created. We saw fretwork being carved, hundreds of identical pieces piled high ready to be woven together into a wall. An entranced man sat rhythmically punching out a winding pattern on a brass platter, all by eye, no lines traced on the surface to help. Thick rugs were built, line by line, hands working in some inconceivable dance across the loom. A finer, intricately patterned cloth, created especially for wedding dresses, had us staring harder as three men stood over a monster loom of strings and wood, caressing it and whacking it to ooze out the fabric, only in this latter dark room were we asked to keep cameras at bay, presumably not to disturb their concentration. Along a wall, two young men occupied themselves twisting yarns together, nails hammered into the mottled plaster their only tools as they ran along, hands flowing with the fine string.

Along a maze-like alleyway we turned into a quite filthy fondouk, once a traveller's rest, it now earned its keep as a leather workshop. Dirty white horses stood on the ground floor, a rope trailed from their front leg to a metal hoop on the wall, while around the courtyard above, men cut coloured leather with broad loose scissors, laughing at the attention as we squeezed past. One of our small band greeted a shoe-maker with Arabic *"es salaam alaykum"*, peace be with you, the young man burst into laughter, red-facing the poor utterer in their attempt to show respect. Further around the corner a more enterprising gentlemen made a game attempt to sell us a beautiful leather footstool, laid flat, awaiting to be fattened with stuffing.

All the work we saw intrigued us, the idea of converting a house in England into a riad with it, at that moment in time, seemed a worthy aim. As our home currently consisted of a two room motorhome, and our dwindling budget dictated when we'd have to return to the reality of working for a living, we had numerous incentives to resist buying everything we saw.

Mohammed was efficient, attempting to show us every aspect of public life in the medina. He wasn't always successful; a foray into a Hammam for the men was repelled by the receptionist in the white-tiled entry room. Unfazed, Mohammed led us around the corner, and one in, one out we stepped into a narrow space. Crude stairs led down into a dark, smoked-filled space, sawdust piled around like butter mountains, we started to sweat within a meter of the door. Among this sat three men, breathing pure wood smoke, taking it in turns to feed armfuls of dust into the glowing mouth of a tall, round, clay furnace. We were looking at the source of the heat for the Hammam steam rooms. One of our group, gave the men a generous tip, and as we walked back into the light, his face was held in genuine anger at the clear discomfort and ill health the smoke breathers would have to endure.

A display of second hand shoes laid out on the floor mystified us as they were stacked in groups of two despite being clearly different. Ah, the lock clicked open, they're the same *size*. There comes a point when practicality outweighs fashion. Gaps in alleyway walls were filled with ripped plastic bags, their decaying contents being scratched over by a multitude of cats. Beggars held out hands, ignored by all but the white Western face. One of the pillars of Islam is to give to those in need, but we didn't give, we didn't want to encourage begging, knowing the local communities would ensure these people survived.

The children, and adults, were getting hungry. Mohammed explained we could take a full meal or a snack somewhere, but either would need to wait. The infamous Fes tanneries were best faced on an empty stomach, he assured us. For the best part of a thousand years, animal hides have been treated here, cleaned of flesh, softened and dyed. And for a thousand years it has stunk. Climbing worn steps inside one of bigger the shops, a bright tunnel of handbags, shoes, belts, jackets, all unsurprisingly rendered from leather, ushers us towards a viewing balcony. A few people stood around, ready to process us through a smooth tradition of gawping and buying. Mint sprigs are handed to us, we sniff them for potency and wonder how bad the stench will be as Mohammed splits the group by language. We're assigned a wide, two-toothed man, clearly a salesmen, as our 'guide'. One of his forlorn ivory stumps wobbled as he spoke, slurring his words, his name was lost to us as he lumbered to the balcony.

The rank air reached us before we saw its source, a deep stench, pervading all like a bass drum beat. Only dimly sickening, maybe helped by the cool January air, we sniffed at the mint and stared out at a thousand years. In that time man has perfected industry, machines distancing them further and further from the act of actually touching the material being worked. Not here. Here nothing has changed but for a disputed introduction of modern chemical dyes. Below us, an artist's pallet of pots are arranged in rows, two wide, filled to varying heights with smooth chocolate browns, blood reds and uninspiring beige. They had an organic, alive look to them, as though some alien race were about to break loose from breeding cocoons.

Men stood partly immersed in the pots, dressed in shorts or trousers dragging at the leather, moving and dropping it as if they're treading it as grapes. One awkward-shaped corner is washed-white, the pots only visible through shadows cast along their rims, a man sat unmoving on a dry ledge wearing a brown top and blue hat stands out in stark contrast. Slowly our eyes work their way upwards away from the scene below. The walls to this bowl of bowls, are haggard, made up from the surrounding workshops, paint flaking away randomly, each one is topped off with fellow camera-wielding gawpers.

Our few-toothed guide explained the canvas-white area was where the hides were cleaned, stripped of hair and softened by soaking in a solution of lime and pigeon excrement. Huge piles of hides were being pulled out of the vats and sat on the side by the workers who balanced on the edges of the vats to work. This was the most dangerous area of the tannery we were told, but the only difference in terms of protective clothing was that the workers here wore long trousers.

The coloured cauldrons were the dyeing vats. We were given a run down of the various plants used to make the different coloured dyes, but the overpowering smell of the horse and donkey urine that the plants were mixed with is the thing we would remember the most. It infused itself in our clothes, seeping around in our van later, it refused to be tamed. Once dyed the hides were hung on the walls of the buildings facing into the courtyard and laid on the surrounding roofs to dry. It had obviously been a yellow dying morning as bright yellow animal shaped hide adorned the buildings like decorations. No machinery was involved.

Our guide explained, once he'd whispered a request for a few Dirhams, that the jobs in the tannery were well paid at up to €250 a month, and therefore sought after. We speculated daily immersion in even natural chemicals would be less than conducive to a ripe old age, and couldn't help but wonder why the process unchanged when the Western world changed by the day. Was it an elaborate show, held in stasis to keep gaping foreigners enthralled? Was all of Fes such a show, all of Morocco? We realised our foolishness; we're a new bunch of invaders, our importance is a passing one, Fes and its tanneries would continue unchanged even with the disappearance of us and the other Euro, Yen and Dollar-toting tourists.

With a few Dirhams in our gummy guide's hand he nodded soberly, approval for us to exit his company. The elderly French couple in our group fingered bright Moroccan slippers behind us, drawing the attention of salespeople, giving us a little time to eye up the hand-crafted, smoothly beautiful workmanship before leaving.

With the seeping stench behind us, a rooftop lunch called, a wide vista of the surrounding roofs enchanting us. The luxurious surroundings were lost on the dog-tired children. Blankets were laid out beside the table, the boys sleeping even when the call to prayer burst from the minarets. We listened in silence, as one by one new callers joined those already singing, building to a city-wide crescendo, before trailing off into the normal level of calls and shouts which pass for silence in Fes. The food consisted of the usual array of tagines, cous-cous, meat and vegetables washed down with soft drinks. The elderly French couple opted for an icing sugar dusted pigeon pie and sticking to stereotype accompanied it with a bottle of wine. An unspoken agreement was made that the cost of Mohammed's meal would be split among the group, which the group only found out about when their bills arrive, but no one complained - he was good company. As the last of the group stood up from the table, an eager cat leapt onto it, to ensure any leftovers were taken care of before the plates were whisked back into the kitchen.

The boys revived, although one was now bleary and crying, Mohammed sensed an experience was needed to entertain them. A bit of fun in a fondouk, fortunately this one was empty of animals, clean and well kept. Just inside the gated entrance, a man-sized set of metal counter-balanced weighing scales hung low, chains holding the flat cups an inch or two off the ground. They were usually used for weighing goods, but we took it in turns to stand on one side of the scales, while a blue coated man with a sports branded baseball cap placed a mix of hexagonal iron and concrete bricks on the other side before declaring our weight. *"Quatre-vingts kilo!"* Having not been on scales for months, 80Kg sounded about right for Jay. He had less luck with the others, but we laughed, and the boys gleamed.

The endless alleyways continued, heads swinging side to side, one tiny room hanging animal skins, even an entire lion complete with roaring head. Legless lizards hung as dried creatures were bunched up for medicinal purposes. Elaborate high-backed wedding seats are stacked, three tiers of steps lifting the bride and groom up high, powerful for a day.

Mohammed waves to us, *"look out for these"*, pointing to a wooden beam at chest height across the alley which forces everyone to duck down. We guessed it was some kind of donkey deterrent device, the explanation was less prosaic. They are there, Mohammed told us, to force people to lower their heads in deference as they approached the Kairaouine Mosque, oh, and also to keep the donkeys away. The mosque is tucked deep in the heart of the medina wedged in, so you can't sense its scale. Mohammed explained that 20,000 people can pray in it at any one time, but being non-Muslim we couldn't go in. We were tired, we didn't mind.

Mohammed was a man used to walking, his energy boundless, but he knew he'd done his job. An archway out into the light brought with it a sudden feeling of space. After hours in the confined, bustling, covered warren, with only the occasional relief of an open square, we felt pleased to be out. Around us stacks of clothes, lucky to pass as rags in England, were piled up for sale, being picked over in earnest. Beyond the clothes the white minibus was parked, the driver sat inside ready to take us home.

Tucked away in the back seats we dozed. Only a plastic-wrapped tray of nougat adorned our backpack, we'd managed to avoid buying anything else. Mohammed had done his job well, the expected immense pressure to buy hadn't materialised, nothing came close. Our day in Fes had furnished us with a delightful and thought provoking taste of Morocco. Topping it off, the price Claude had told us was for two people, not per person as we had assumed. Thanking Mohammed with a good tip, he tipped his head in thanks to us before we all walked, as a group for the last time, across the campsite. Our pace quickened as we approached Dave, remembering prisoner pooch who had been cooped up for nearly eight hours. Opening Dave's door, Charlie flung himself towards us in a wriggle of fur then headed off out of the door for a sniff around and a wee. As Jay fussed him guiltily, Julie inspected the Dave's insides, all clear, no mishaps.

WALT DISNEY CAMPING

In a no-man's land between Fes and the countryside, stands a prefabricated part of Europe. The *Marjane* supermarket chain has entered the vernacular of those wandering Morocco, as its goods are all priced and it sells sought-after alcohol, among other things. This grey box stood alone, the familiar retail park of Europe having failed to materialise around it. Dave parked on the edge of an almost empty car park and we walked in, taking note of an oversized sign above us, enforced by uniformed guards: *no photos*. Inside we stepped back into Spain, France and Britain. To our right, a cash machine, a relief since old Fes had a dearth of them, we imagined everyone in the medina either had no money, or kept it stuffed in a foot stool or mattress. Just along from the cash machine stood a line of gleaming motorbikes, the same simple ubiquitous type which, battered and worn, ply the streets across the country. Each one represented several year's wages for many of the rustic workers we saw from our cab.

We entered through the turnstiles with a different cadence to our step. Julie stepped in lightly, eager to search out the differences which would make this place entirely separate to our life-long shopping experiences. Jay plodded, the place felt false, the antithesis of the tiny floor-to-ceiling stacked, unpriced shops in the real world outside that had provoked such sweet, tingling fear.

Flat panel televisions, tall white fridges, microwaves and electric kettles? Our adventure felt diminished, Europe suddenly caught up with us. The books section drew us back out to Africa, Arabic scripted, placed backwards on the shelves since they were read from the rear pages first. The food isles were gently patrolled by uniformed hostesses, seemingly outnumbering the shoppers, answering questions and holding out samples of food.

A sparrow darted from the roof space, nipping at a grain on the polished floor. The prices fascinated us, our memories quickly filling with the benchmark figures we sought to help us avoid foolishness in the unpriced places to come. They seemed high, the same or more as we paid in Spain, how could anyone here afford them? Looking up, only the well-heeled and the foreign shared the isles. Our metal trolley, wheels disappointingly steering well, held a few items, pastries, long-life milk, a cake or two, a bag of intriguing chicken spice, things chosen more by price than need.

Just past the fresh fruit section, a self-contained afterthought: alcohol. Seeming to expand beyond the boundary of the building the area was surrounded by walls on three sides. The alcohol buyers appeared furtive, not helped by the small separate check-outs leading past cross-armed guards out to a slightly open, unglazed side door. Cans and bottles were dropped dirty into white, plain plastic bags for obvious but hidden transport to the cars parked nearby out under the gaze of the sun. Curiosity drew us in, although our cupboards remained well-enough stocked to put off this small test for another time. A combination of familiar brands and the unknown, all universally expensive. Now we realised why Arthur was so keen to buy our Spanish wine, he got it for a fraction of the going rate.

At the checkout a familiar faux-pas, bags of fresh fruit and familiar-looking vegetables should have been weighed and labelled. The operator sat unhurried, as though dealing with dallying businessmen waiting to climb aboard Concorde. Jay dashed back embarrassed to a previously unseen staff member, who took them and passed them back stickered with prices.

With new purchases slotted into still bulging cupboard crevices, we could no longer put off the road south. It was time to confront the images of little skiing men sprinkled along our route. Quickly the traffic left us, and soon the red line on our map, tracing our three hour route, intersects a single white dot, the small one-donkey cluster of shops and houses not deserving a named mention, but requiring us to slow to a crawl. Daring to briefly take our eyes off the road ahead, both of us working in unison to spot gaps, potholes, people and creatures, we glanced sideways. Sat around on haphazard bunches of rickety seats, leaning against walls or sat on haunches, men would do nothing. They sipped at tea and smoked, while women carried water, sticks and other massive unidentified loads. The multi-featured and expensive pushchairs and prams of Europe didn't exist, babies and toddlers were held tight to their mother's backs using only cloth.

The air grew cooler, and the country around us grew more barren, gatherings of trees stood together against deserts of stone. Our progress was slow, a continual stream of overtaking taxis, vans and a single frightening, vast, wind-shoving tourist coach slotting into the gap in front. At times it felt as if we were in reverse as we sought to maintain some semblance of a braking distance. Snow huddled into the shadows of trees, and with it came a new sight. Stood alone on upright stones, or hanging from trees, old label-less containers, an engine oil shaped one here, cooking oil there. Evenly spaced, the curious sight went on and on, marking out each side of the route like roadworks. Mostly unmanned, some would be held aloft by eager faces, arms dropping dejected in our rear mirrors. Eventually a scrawled sign demystified the scene: *miel*, honey.

A rare queue of traffic on a climbing, curving section of road leading into the town of Ifrane provided entertainment. One after another, cars would pull into the temporarily traffic free lane, drive as fast and as far as they could before, just about to precipitate a face-first collision, they tucked back into a non-existent gap in the queue. No horns snorted anger, no vulgar hand gestures demanded vengeance, no doors flew open to cough out an enraged wrench-bearer. What to make of it? It seemed some simply felt the queue didn't apply to their status, and those being pushed back agreed.

Ifrane, pronounced eefrane, is a new town, built by the French in 1929 as a place for the patricians to hide from the summer heat, independence saw it slowly transferred to the Moroccans. Nicknamed *Little Switzerland*, it doesn't belong, any more than a Marjane supermarket would sit within the medina walls of Fes. When the first sign of it appeared to us, a chimneyed, yellow stone-walled alpine style chalet, we knew we'd climbed into the Middle Atlas Mountains. The snow grew bolder, the low slopes to either side of us evenly covered, now only small melted patches, like a cheetah's spots, revealed the earth beneath. The town announced itself with a giant advertising hoarding, no words or logos, the suited King's enigmatic smile peering down from a gold encrusted throne, the Moroccan star above him.

Our intention to stop and inspect Ifrane closer, looking for the inevitable tricks in the illusion, was thwarted. The place was throbbing with visitors, police directed traffic away from a large car park, already full. A crowd of Moroccans crossed the road heading for a garden area. We guessed Ifrane draws people as a novelty, an alien place and with all the fresh snow it was a big draw today. To us it was a mirage of the familiar, so we drove on.

Looking back from the road out of town, an island of red-roofed two story, creamy apartment blocks floated among the snow white covered rock. We guessed this was the once-shanty part of town, where those serving the needs of the upper-class protectors lived. As the road continued cars slipped purposefully onto side lanes. Adults and children, warmed with new knitted hats and scarves, long coats and boots, messed around in the snow. A squeal marked the direct hit of a snowball, fun in lands where the white stuff is a nuisance, exclusive fun in Morocco. We marvelled at the sight, and worried that the dry road might yet trap us, or worse propel us with locked wheels off into the stones.

A coloured arrow on the map depicted a camping castle by the road. Our friends Chris and Tina had named it '*Walt Disney Camping*' when they passed through earlier, but declined to tell us why, we'd need to see it for ourselves they said. An incredible, crenelated fortress in even, yellow stone blocks topped with tiled cones stood solidly, demanding the question *"what on Earth?"*. We slowed Dave and, staring in disbelief, drove straight past the entrance, a high arch straddled by two protective circular towers alongside which sat two golden urns, large enough to swallow much of our passing home. We weren't ready to accept this was a campsite, but when nothing else materialised on the horizon we turned around, and pulled up the lego-studded pathway under the arch. A barrier requested we stop, a guard sat at a small table in the shade. Climbing out, we found our shared pool of French words more of a shallow puddle, but the barrier was raised, accompanied by pointing and miming which we pretended to understand. Before we drove on we were presented with a bumper sticker showing the entrance to the site, evidence to stare at should we wake and wonder if it was all a dream.

The bobbled roadway continued, curving up the hill, like a rich child's playground for his battery-powered car. The entrance was only the beginning, more huge, brand new towers and walls leaned over us, a market area over here, a series of posh bungalows over there. Signs, neatly printed by machine, drew the iconic outline of a motorhome, and pointed us further up the hill. The place made us hypocrites after the Fes supermarket. A sign pointed us in the direction of *Business Class*, maybe tongue-in-cheek but for us it was just that. An empty, flattened area of the hill, a panoramic view over the valley, and only a single, friendly, Dutch motorhome for a neighbour. From our vantage point we could see the whole site. A tall wall topped with decorative moon-like orbs among clawing foliage, wrapped around as the road climbed high up the steep hillside behind us, surely a space for tents as no motorhome could venture there.

We gleefully took in the sight of European luxuries. An eager inspection revealed a spanking new shower block; doors, shower heads and hot water all there, all in place, hardly any insects to get Julie jumping: *hooray*! A large area set out to enable us to dump our burgeoning waste water tank: *get in*! Electrical power points inside water-proof boxes, the act of plugging Dave in requiring no bravery: *you beauty*! Beside a pond, white ducks, deep red chickens and a fluffy white tailed rabbit flapped, scratched and hopped. Charlie would need to be restrained! Small patches of snow around us, joining to form a solid ring on the hill above the upper wall, spelt a cold night to come. Dave's LPG tank was brimming from a last-minute fill-up in Spain as we knew it couldn't be bought in Morocco. The blown-air heating it powers was left on low to heat the water tank and the cupboard holding our water heater, so we feared no frost damage. Our halogen electric heater was plugged in and glowed like a small sun to keep us all toasty warm.

Eating our dinner in Dave we look out over the bare-chested hills, obscured in places the grey, feathery, lifeless branches of trees, planted around the site. In the distance the round copper-green roof of a mosque stood partnered with a square towering minaret. The crescent topping the minaret is silhouetted against the clear sky and setting sun. A knock on the door brings the offer of bread from the campsite, after our supermarket visit we're stocked up so we decline. After dinner we take an evening stroll within the comforting walls of the site, the stack of loaves left next to the empty restaurant told us the price we'd have been charged: *free*. Chris and Tina later told us how they were wowed with an entire meal, at no charge.

Feigned attacks from Charlie noisily scattered the ducks, chickens and rabbits as we passed the pond, the upper level of the site drawing us, the sign humorously pointing upwards to *First Class*. Devoid of any motorhomes, the second, perfect shower block was closed. The chemical toilet emptying point was built inside a tower which featured a wobbling metal staircase to a viewing platform. We held tight, climbing one at a time unsure if it would take the weight of both of us. Standing agape at the view over the valley, we wondered at the economics of such an opulent place, all but empty. To our left perhaps stood the answer, a house, little more than a shack, the owner in black boots, trekking downhill on a donkey with his child holding on in front of him. The money we would pay to stop here, by our European benchmark, was little, by local standards, one night was two week's wages for the poorest around us.

As the night cooled in around us, encouraged by the evening call to prayer, we watched the stars blaze until our necks ached drinking mint tea, made from bags we'd bought at Marjane, a shadow of the real thing. We could feel the country growing on us. In a few short days, our standards had been challenged to the point we laughed at ourselves: those considered poor in our country only have one second-hand car. An economic disaster slashes millions from bank accounts of the rich, leaving them with mere millions.

A MONKEY ATE MY BREAKFAST

The next morning, the cloudless sky had drained the softness from the earth. We crunched across frozen patches of snow, enjoying the sensation, before filling the chilled air with steam from copious amounts of hot water in the showers, dressing awkwardly afterwards in record time. Our Dutch neighbour raved about the brilliance of a site she'd stayed at in Midelt, another mysterious name on our map. It was the right distance away along our red road south, so we asked Shat-nav to find us a route to Midelt, the request being more to justify buying her the maps, rather than any actual need. The road network in Morocco fans out like a blood supply, thinning to nothing at the edges, criss-crossed only with the unsealed tracks, on our map white lines representing the tracks were simply labelled *piste*.

Before leaving, Dave was fettled: water and loo waste dropped into comfortably official and obvious facilities. With a hundred litres of fresh water loaded into the on-board tank, we almost felt like adventurers, *bring on the desert, we have our own oasis*. The misunderstood mime of the site guard yesterday became clear: we needed to visit the office to pay.

Julie stepped inside, a smiling lady greeted her in French. Next to her desk a collection of tiny birds sang out a backing-track from their cages. Paying and thanking the lady Julie grinned as she returned to Dave, the price for our stay in Disneyesque luxury? Around half the price of the ill-maintained, shower-in-the van, transit camps we'd been to further north, a trend which continued as we headed south towards the desert.

Approaching the exit barrier, we needed help from the guard. We knew that the cedar forests around the campsite are home to wild monkeys, but we didn't know where the best place was to see them. The guard was caught a little off guard as we asked him: *"Ou sont les singes, s'il vous plait?"*. His face wrinkled as he tried to work out what we'd said, Jay put him out of his misery with a goofy monkey impression, coupled with congruous noises, it had him smiling. He pointed to the right and wrote on a scrap of paper; *2 km, Cèdre Gouraud Foret*.

The Middle Atlas Mountains house around three quarters of the world's population of Barbary Macaques, the same monkeys famous for thieving picnics and causing havoc on Gibraltar rock. While around 300 live and thrive on free sandwiches on Gibraltar, in North Africa the estimated numbers of around 21,000 are declining; in 2009 they were declared endangered.

The single track road alongside the sign was sealed, Dave would easily pass it. With no idea just how far away our furry fanged friends were, we headed towards the tall trees, alone on the road. Swinging left, a narrow wooden bridge appeared, worryingly blocked at the far end by a group of men holding the reigns of camels, and horses wearing richly embroidered saddles.

Feeling unsure of protocol, we crawled onwards, and the men simply eased themselves and their charges off the bridge, staring at us but with no other response. The sealed road didn't reappear and the snow and ice-packed mud ahead panicked us. Turning the light-steering Dave under a tree, a tentative brake press brought home to a halt. Jumping out, the ground was a muddied ice rink, maybe we were stuck, but we might as well hunt out the monkey before we attempted to find out.

Taking one of our old bikes from the rack on Dave's rear, Jay slithered about riding up the rutted path, checking the remaining distance to the animals, if indeed they felt like appearing in this weather. A little way up the incline the track opened up into a clearing, a series of small wooden huts lining the sides of it, most of them firmly shut, yet outside the few that were open locals sat around, unusually paying no attention to a potential punter. No monkeys. Maybe they were high up in the trees? An aimless ride around found nothing, no noise, no beasts. Back in the clearing, the unexpectedly useful monkey searching phrase, minus the accompanying impression, was tried on a group of three men. One of them slowly turned his body sideways and lifted his arm, pointing: *"la bas?"*. How does a man miss a monkey sat less than ten meters away? Ask Jay.

A few minutes later, Julie was rescued from a baseless fear of hassle she'd anticipated from the horse and camel group, and the bike was replaced on its rack. Figuring that dogs and monkeys probably don't mix well, Charlie was left and safely locked in Dave. A few Dirhams, too many judging from his quickly-hidden beam, were handed to the man who'd acquired the status of *le Guardien* by donning a high-visibility vest, before we trudged through the cool thick mud back to the clearing. More of the troop had made an entrance, or maybe they were there all along. Big, yawning males reminding us with fangs of their status as wild, untamed, and able to defend themselves. Tiny babies clung to females, while cheeky adolescents threw themselves fearlessly from branch to branch, no tails with which to balance.

Universally thick-furred, brown, black and grey-white, it was clear how they withstood the freeze. We stood and laughed, searching for a clue of emotion in their faces, while keeping a safe distance. A sedan car, risking being beached, wheel span to a stop down the hill and a smartly-dressed Moroccan family tip-toed through the mire. Producing packaged cup cakes from a bag, the monkeys squealed in anticipation and coolly reached for the free lunch. The easy and smooth opening and unwrapping, with the monkey not even looking at the expected puzzle, demonstrated they were very used to cupcakes. A catalyst for us, what could we feed them. Julie had put a banana in our rucksack for a late breakfast, being unsure how long the walk up to the monkeys would be; perfect. One of the males' keen gaze saw the banana appear and he brazenly walked over on all fours towards Jay. Sitting with legs held tightly together, he calmly reached for the half-peeled fruit. No retreat necessary, he was clearly comfortable with the scenario, he sat and peeled the fruit, ripping away the remaining skin with bright white fearsome teeth before eating. Julie brought us both back to reality: *"hang on a minute, that monkey just ate my breakfast!".*

Charlie sniffed at us accusingly back in Dave, and we felt victorious. Looking over at the group of men stood with the high visibility clad *Guardien*, attempting to warm themselves by a one-stick fire, we gave them oranges. They looked at each other wondering whether to accept until one thanked us, and passed them out around the group, these were proud men. They paid us back immediately as Dave's front wheels span on the ice rendering us stationary, pushing hard they moved us onto the unfrozen ground away from the trees, walking away without waving.

We crossed the Middle Atlas Mountains, a little at a time. The road bucked and weaved, but these were tame hills by driving standards, with none of the cliff-brushing overhangs, or toothpaste tube squeezing constrictions of the northern Spanish mountains. A heavy yellow truck passed on the other side of the road, an orange snowplough attached, the paint rubbed away. Rough muted green and brown fields to either side of us made the snow plough look foolish, but perhaps the Middle Atlas might bite us after all? The premonition drew closer to reality as the trees gave up, leaving the road a ribbon of grey grip through a slippery white wilderness. We grabbed our sunglasses as the blinding African light scattered from every surface, the snow grew thicker. Passing snow gates, their simple barrier standing perpendicular to the road; it was clear the road was open. The empty sky had nothing new to add to the landscape today but illumination, dialled up to high.

The land to our right rose up in a wave above Dave, marking the top of a col, we saw scenes from our childhoods. Cars abandoned in favour of wooden sleighs, plastic sheets, old bags, anything slippery, children and adults alike were climbing the hill and hurtling down. A lady in robes and head scarf, erupted into a uncontrolled full length cry of joy as she barrelled along. We near-shouted at each other when we spotted a skier, wearing a brand new pink jacket, unblemished white boots, loping along the flat with matching poles. Among the cars we saw people prostrate in prayer, bending their heads to the ground on mats placed over the snow. In contrast, as the snow became natural again, unpacked, a group of three men stood and dug, their tractor and trailer stuck fast.

Without knowing it, we'd topped out in the Middle Atlas, the road now steadily sloped downwards, and the vista caused us to take breath. A coffee-stained scrub land stretched off, only piste roads smoothed the surface in parallel tracks, bending back and forth around dry river beds and knuckles of land. Before the distant horizon could meet the pure blue sky, however, it had to meet and surmount a formidable obstacle. Mountains, real solid, dangerous ones. Devoid of the jagged grey peaks of the Italian Dolomites, this massif made up for it in sheer bulky presence, punching a space for itself between heaven and earth. The High Atlas Mountains, spread wide across our view, must have appeared insurmountable to the timid among those before us, those like us but without a map or a diesel-powered home on wheels. These mountains would provide our backdrop for the next few days, drawing us towards them.

Even here, among this plain, dead desert, goats and sheep were herded. The dust and soil must provide nutrition enough through unseen blades of grass or other scrawny plants to keep the animals alive. Raised for both wool and their meat, they would be sold for local consumption in Midelt. Counter to common sense, the price of meat is highest in wettest seasons, the abundance of feeding making the animals easier to keep alive. When the rain fails to come, rather than lose valuable income, the animals are sold for slaughter. Life here is tough. Donkeys hop on one free front leg, searching for green, their other leg tethered. Despite the cruelty of this method of restraint, it beat being dead. The carcass of an unfortunate donkey lay where it had fallen, being tugged at by a wild dog, the unwelcome image imprinting itself on Julie. Jay's attempt to lighten the mood, life here not being dog eat dog, but dog eat donkey, fell on deaf ears.

We passed through a couple of small towns on the wide open plain. One of them was pretty much a huge red and white painted telecoms mast, a slim skeleton pyramid scratching at the sky. The dwellings here appeared to have risen from the earth around them, small and square, flat roofed, prevented from blending in by the obligatory off-white curving plate of a satellite dish. In a larger, livelier town, a market closed the road down to a tunnel between the flowing crowd. Generation-old vans stood still at angles, with empty black roof racks. Pick up trucks with wooden fences added around the sides to keep in livestock, poured their contents out for sale. We carefully shoved at the crowd, edging along, keeping momentum and avoiding the wide cloth umbrellas carried in defence of the sun. At the exit to each town, the last buildings formed a stage curtain, drawing back proudly to unveil the drama. The High Atlas a shadow-speckled sky-high wall of pale blue rock and ice above the narrowing plain, no break or weakness visible.

The town of Midelt welcomed us before the peaks, a place to rest from the demands of the Moroccan roads, putting off the mountain ascent for a day. Our Dutch neighbour the previous evening had given us directions to the municipal campsite, amid a screech of enthusiasm which bent us backwards a little in retreat. Her directions were simple, reflecting the basic nature of the town, *"past the bus station, left at the roundabout, then right"*. When we told her the price of the campsites we'd visited in the north, her eyes grew wider: punctuated by flailing arms her advice hit us like an errant football: *"go to Midelt, it's cheap!"*.

Crawling through the town in search of the campsite, the directions partly forgotten, we craned our necks to see the storks balanced high on unlikely balls of sticks atop of buildings. Inanimate, they stood framed against the pure blue sky. Distracted, the town camping nearly escaped the weight of our home. Oddly relieved to fall back into Moroccan reality, the campsite would be better titled a high walled car park. But for the presence of another motorhome, we'd have questioned whether this was our target. By the entrance stood an ageing, bulbous-nosed, flat-tyred truck, looking like something that had dropped in from a 1950s mid-western US state. Opposite it, white-robed waiters carefully positioned chairs around tables, both similarly decked in white cloth, preparing for a celebration dinner. Glasses stood in ranks alongside silver plates, decorated in swirling patterns.

A cat waiting beneath a table for scraps became impatient, sauntering to the truck, an effortless leap was rewarded with a spot to soak up the sun.

A gentle knock at Dave's window shifted our focus back to where we were. *Le Guardien*, an unlikely title for a man who's hands were clearly only made for peaceful shaking, stood in ancient clothes. Passing us an infinitely photocopied sheet of paper, his version of the official registration forms, he waved away our attempt to locate a pen, and drifted off again, *no problem, give it to me tomorrow, no problem*. Walking out of the campsite, Charlie huffed and stretched for the cat sunbathing on the truck, a comical sight as it royally ignored him. Men arrived in clean, new cars, Arabic on the registration plates seemed misplaced, filling all spaces in the car park of a campsite. Greeting each other with handshakes, the men quietly joined the celebration, no women arrived.

While touring the myriad of exotic things in the souks of Fes we'd seen woollen Berber blankets being made. With limited cash on us and the knowledge that the medinas of Fes and Marrakech were expensive places to buy from, we'd abstained. Driving through Midelt to the campsite it became clear that this was a plain town, a working place, hardly a foreign tourist trap, so we might pick up a bargain. Repeating the name of our prey: *couverture en lainne*, we embarked on our hunt for the small souk mentioned in our guidebook. Passing a post office we were reminded of the need to post a birthday card home. We hadn't seen cards for sale anywhere since we'd arrived in the country, so one would have to be made. The stamp we needed to send it would be harder to buy than we naively thought, the post office was closed and only opened for two hours per day.

Walking back around the roundabout, and towards the bus station, the footfall thickened, confirming we'd found the town centre. Through a yellowing window a stack of bright fleece blankets announced a candidate for our Dirhams. Entering Moroccan shops felt to us like leaping into a deep, dark pool from a great height. A long breath, unwittingly drawn in, readying ourselves for the unknown, no hesitation at the doorway or we wouldn't go in. There was no need here, there was no big sell, the owners were gentle souls. The *"bonjour, hello, guten tag"* shouts, or simple whistles as if to a dog of Fez were absent. None of the age-old encouragements were called out at us: *"look, no buy!"*, *"buy, no look!"* (this novel one almost worked; we laughed and shook the caller's hand), *"come see, come see!"*, *"I do you good price!"*.

We visited a carpet shop, and accidentally another robe shop on our search that day, all of the sellers felt genuine and trustworthy, suggesting places which might sell what we were after. In the final shop as they realised what we wanted, they advised us: to get a wool blanket, you need to go to the convent, they make them there. We picked out the word *Myriem* as they gave directions, pointing along the road. A shiver announced the imminent evening, our journey to the convent would have to wait until the morning.

Our walk back to Dave, heads tilted towards the smooth mountains glimpsed between concrete buildings, was punctuated by two events. The first entirely passive, a walled military base with only a little more protection than the campsite, explained a earlier-heard trumpeting. The second shook us. Inside a builder's yard two dogs lay in the sun, a few meters back from the scrappy roadside pathway. As we passed them Julie noticed one of the dogs stand and stalk towards us. Charlie wasn't unaware either, immediately collapsing to one side as the animal silently launched itself towards him. It's jaws clamped shut on the air recently vacated by our dog's hairless belly. Julie's reaction came as swift as the attack. Arms flung out she released an enraged yawp before it had chance to strike again. Heads turned along the street as she chased the previously demonic mutt back into the yard, where it slunk into a corner.

Charlie rolled back onto his feet, and tried to resume sniffing for scraps. We picked him up and held him, finding no physical marks of damage, as the people along the street stared. From that point onwards, all Moroccan dogs took on a new meaning to us. Already aware of their status as guard dogs, we actually understood what it meant: any approach in or near to their area would result in sharp-toothed attack. The defence proved simple enough, following the lead of locals, picking up a stick or stone scattered entire packs of encroaching wild dogs, without any need to actually throw. We crossed over the road to ensure maximum distance in case of canine retaliation, as the adrenalin soaked away; at the roadside the dusty black lifeless shape of a puppy further reminded us where we were.

Early mornings were already our norm, our excited minds calmed through exhaustion during the night again raced with the sunrise. Julie pulled at a cupboard, card and thick felt pens magically appeared and a card fashioned itself *"Happy Birthday from Africa!"*. Next stop, the post office. A tall, dark-skinned man stood on the steps outside, hands held still alongside his robe, he watched us silently. Jay looked inside, turned around, and gave a thumbs-down to a waiting Julie and Charlie. The small room was lined with benches, each of which was crammed, a paper ticketing system used for fairness. Two hours of service per day looked like only a few of the crowd would be served. We left in what we hoped to be the right direction for the convent. Within a few hundred meters a post box stood outside a shop selling newspapers and stationery. Scanning the window, the word *timbres* loudly shouted out from a dinner-plate sized sticker, *stamps*. We bought one, legitimised the envelope with it, and sent it on its way. We would get news of its safe arrival, eventually.

The road to the blanket-laden convent sank below sloped sides of dry earth and stones. Charlie's nose twitched and his lead yanked back and forth as though a desperate, powerful fish were attached. The guilty scraps of food, fluttering thin plastic bags and general detritus laid where it was flung or ushered by the wind. A lack of traffic eased our walk along single-lane sections of road, between yellow-rendered houses. Child architects with a crayon could sketch out these dwellings. A simple rabble of boxes, some topped off with hand-patted mud walls, all sporting a thin forest of high-poled aerials peering off in all directions, no consensus on the source of favourite TV programmes. A mosque alongside the route felt more a part of the sky than the ground which founded it. Smooth beige sides and squared green circles forming wide-stepped ladders around the minaret. We were looking for a convent though, a Christian place, a confusion to us in this clearly Islamic land.

Convent Myriem, stands within the compound of the Notre Dame de l'Atlas Monastery. The monastery is a refuge, the monks moved to it following an attack on their place of worship in Algeria in which several of their group were kidnapped, some were killed. The nuns in the convent are tolerated by the locals through their continual efforts to help the community, teaching valuable crafts to the local women. As we worked out which part of the building was the convent, two girls followed us from a distance. Sensing we were about to walk through the doorway, one of them called to us, asking if we had pencils or sweets, *"bonjour, stylo, bonbon?"*.

An incident on the road to Midelt shaped our response: stopping to photograph the mountains, a group of boys walked over to Dave. The first arrived, a real urchin, face dirty and sleeves too long, and stuck out a hand *"bonbon"*, a demand, not a question. Jay handed him a few sweets, turning to the next boy. *"Zizziz"* the first boy demanded, thrusting his hand out again having pocketed the first harvest, his face stern, a tiny threat. Turning quickly angry and embarrassed, Jay demand that he give the sweets back was refused with a quick head shake, and the hand thrust up and down, pumping at chest height.

That was the first and final time we gave out sweets or pencils, the boy hardened us. We knew that children here could earn more begging than their fathers did in their chosen, productive craft, and while the latest King had expressed his desire for all children to be educated, albeit with too-few schools to meet the need, foreigners handing over sweets, pens or worse money would easily poison this aim. Our experience on that day underlined it.

The girls disappeared as the door to the convent opened, a woman stepped slowly out, only her stature and location giving her away as a nun. A few shared words of French confirmed we were at the right place, and Charlie was OK to enter. With smiling eyes and an inviting arm, she ushered us though a disappointingly normal door. The room pressed in on us, we were immediately surrounded. Against three walls, Moroccan women, wrapped in colourful robes, sat huddled on low chairs, eyes down, focussed on the white cloth in their laps and the embroidery needles in their hands. Hidden glances at Charlie were the only indication that we were more than ghosts. Coloured threads caught the light, a small gas heater tried in vain to warm the room. A hip-high wooden table ran along the only empty wall, a single lady sat by it, white fabric stretched out in front of her.

Our nun, we discovered quickly, was an accomplished tour guide. Her hands placed us into the only corner of the room with space for the three of us, by the door-less entry to the next room. Charlie's attempts to map this new environment with his pulsating black nose were cut short, as we commanded him to sit, relieved when he obeyed. The nun placed her hands together and began a monologue, with more relief the words reached us in English. She explained how they were inspired by the spirit of St. Francis of Assisi, who during a crusade in 1219 met with the Muslim Sultan of Egypt in an unprecedented gesture of dialogue and peace. A few Franciscan nuns came to Midelt in 1926 and established a convent shortly afterwards. They maintained a profound respect for the Muslim faith, we were told, and a desire to collaborate with their Muslim neighbours. In evidence, they set up an embroidery and weaving workshop for the local women who could learn the skill, earn some additional income for their families and also learn to read and write. As the years went on they also opened an orphanage, a dispensary, and a primary school.

Reaching down to a set of hands working nimbly at the cloth, she stayed them with a touch. Turning the cloth over a few times, back and forth, she explained the pattern was double-sided. No threads hung loose. *"Look closely"*, we leaned in, ignoring Charlie who had started to whine, *"they use no lines to guide them"*. Incredibly intricate, symmetrical patterns; some as large as a table were being sewn in place by eye. We started to grasp the art and skill as the nun's script continued; a woman would complete a four year apprenticeship before anything they produced was sold. The workforce and apprentices totalled around 75 women, with the number fluctuating as life circumstances changed. Some women had Friday off for prayers, some Sunday, others worked from home so they could raise their children. We met a woman who was in her third year of apprenticeship, she smiled at us, uneasy at the attention, immediately moving back to work after acknowledging us. She was helping to teach the others and working out on squared paper how to fit a pattern around a corner of a tablecloth.

As the nun gestured to us to move through the doorway, we nodded our heads at the women, shy ego-less looks and smiles returned. The next room was equally crammed with women, we drew back in discomfort, realising that Moroccans don't have the luxury of our wide boundaries of British personal space. The seven people in a taxi had shown us this, four faces turned backwards as they overtook, a toot-toot of thanks for pulling over. Here in this small space we felt it.

In this second room, women who had completed the apprenticeship created beauty. Again, all but ignoring us their hands worked confidently over a canvases of fine white and cream material. Charlie immediately resumed whining and by instinct the ladies looked up, faces turning to the nun for approval. After a nod of consent, they stopped work, bending to stroke his back, giggling. To the back of the room sat looms, as usual their cascade of strings impossibly intricate. The wool is bought by the convent raw, in sacks, straight from the sheep's back. The ladies wash it in the river, spin, dye and weave it into bright, soft and tough rugs. We ran fingers over a carpet hanging completed on a wall and asked how long it would take to make. The nun thought about it, this wasn't part of the script *"this one, about a month, for two women"*. The nun left us for a moment and the lingering wonder of worth lifted to the surface, no mention had been made of value. *"Two skilled woman, one month, say sixty day's work"*, without a cigarette packet we worked in the air. *"Say they earn £3 an hour, that's £180, plus the cost of the wool and the overheads, and then profit, maybe £250?"*. We never asked how much the women earned, but the next room answered queries on costs.

This last room was announced as the display room, serving a dual purpose of displaying the finery, and inviting you to buy it. Small tables and stools displayed completed cushion covers, tablecloths, napkins and handkerchiefs, walls papered with scarves, rugs and blankets. The artwork was faultless, and of almost zero interest to us, none of it resembled the soft, simple blankets we'd seen in Fes. The nun, having completed the tour, took her leave and we reached for the hanging cardboard tags. Staring at the neat pencil figures, our maths temporarily failing us, we were taken aback at how reasonable they were. Then a moment of realisation increased the prices by a factor of ten. Ah, the two cushion covers we held slowly placed themselves back onto the small pile. As the nun came back into the room, looking at us in expectation, we explained it was all beautiful and great quality, but not our style. We wanted to contribute of course, and passed over a note, which she accepted with a smile, not even looking at it. Julie handed over several boxes of the coloured pencils we'd bought in Algeciras, explaining how we hoped they would be of use in the school. The nun thanked us and placed them into a cupboard along with the money. She then showed us slowly back through the workshops. We breathed a joint sigh of relief as the doorway closed behind us.

While we prepared Dave for our days drive, movement from a side window caught our eye. We watched intermittently as we shuffled various items back into their cupboards. The elderly, French couple - owners of the campsite's only other motorhome, an outline map of Europe on its side, the coloured-in countries exhibiting their travel experience, were talking with *le Guardien*. He stood passively, arms at his side, as the French man took a large blue plastic box from one of the many locker doors in his van. Missing the next few moments, our attention diverted back inside, we looked back out to see the *guardien's* holed shoes sitting abandoned, his feet now feeling their way around a pair of second hand white trainers. With his back to us we could still see his smile as he hugged the couple one by one. They seemed unmoved, as though it was a simple duty they had performed, and placed the plastic box back into their van.

THE OASIS

The road bent eastwards, turning parallel to the mass of the mountains, as if afraid to tackle them. Behind us the Middle Atlas Mountains rolled out of view, red and pale, embarrassed by their southerly neighbours. The plain spread before us, as if a giant hand had scooped at the earth, cutting away all height. Tough bushes which had added a mop of green outside Midelt gave up the hopeless act of growth, the plain a flat pit of pale dust. Rocks lay around, appearing sharp edged, freshly calved from some unseen mothering massif.

The mountains rose up to our right, the snow melted from their feet. As we searched for a way over, the solid ridge became two ranks, revealing a lower route between them. The road also spotted this and turned to head for the gap, uplifted. Gears dropped, fifth to fourth, to third. Foot-high concrete barriers between us and the drop-off were comforting as we lifted skywards, freshly painted white, their tops lined with a warning red. The views became dangerous, turning our heads to the north to gasp at the ungraspable beauty. Carefully picking its way along the contours of the lower slopes, the road cleverly and thankfully avoided the cooler heights and their snow. Squared-off Arabic letters extolling the greatness of Allah across a roadside hill made up the only patches of white.

Passing a col, the road dropped away at a gentle pace on the other side, into lower hills. The snow flashed in our rear view mirrors confirming we were through, the high peaks giving way to mere mounds, rippled as though part of the bed of an ancient sea. Lone donkeys trod between the rocks, the entire world a path, carrying someone and a sack or two from nowhere to nowhere. Square buses stood along the road, doors swung wide open, uneven canvas tied down onto their roof racks. A shining patch of water appeared, with a backdrop of a town of mud, itself overshadowed by a ragged earth hill. The trees failed to live up to the stereotype of wafting palms, but nevertheless, this was our first oasis.

The words *Gorges du Ziz* were carved onto a pale stone plaque, contrasting against the deep red rocks it was mounted on, above them in italics *Tunnel du Legionnaire*. Whilst we love maps, the flowing lines of roads each hide a thousand stories, the coloured paper as much representing the land as a limerick captures the feeling of enduring love. Water to our right poured along an ancient pathway, cutting a canyon with million-year patience. Giant rocks, tumbled under its soft, never ending caress, lay belly-up, waiting to be devoured.

On the other side of the short, rough-sided tunnel, hacked by French Legionnaires, we reached a rare area of spare land beside the road, its location the perfect place to capture the sight. Dave's handbrake clicked on, and we jumped from the door, Julie drawn to the edge to frame the shots. We'd heard people could appear from nowhere in these deserts, our man took a minute or two to materialise. His call of 'bonjour' spun Jay around in surprise, well aware of our remoteness. He smiled, lifting up a green plaited likeness of a camel, complete with two round carrying baskets at its sides. *"Non, merci, nous n'avons pas d'enfants"* failed to deflect him; these items were not just for children, they were multi-purpose. A long loop attached to the camel made it equally suited to hanging from a rear-view mirror, pointing the way. As he held up the souvenir, Jay saw the seller's hands. Cracked, hard and bent, it would be a surprise if he could still make these items himself. A quick haggle and the camel jumped into the van with Julie who had begun her tactical retreat when the sale began.

More men appeared, younger, eagerly thrusting identical camels, shouting, held back by the original camel man. As Jay reached for Dave's door, camel man tried his luck: *"Vous avez de la biere?"*. Leaving the door open, Jay took two beers, cooling in our fridge, and handed them to him, it might be winter but it was still hot under the glaring sun. The face looking back was aghast, maybe waiting for a price to be named, we closed the door and pulled off, happy. The beer, we knew, was worth ten times the amount we haggled off the price and as we drove away we saw the man hand one of the cans to a friend, both looking at us as we passed out of sight.

As the grey edgeless road cut through rock and dust, our camel swung back and forth, a green fleck against desolation. We named it the swing-o-meter, its new role in life was to visually represent the bumps we could feel on the road, like a humped G-force indicator. Floating along, our windscreen and side windows three clumsy panels giving the illusion of movement, the only clue we were still in contact with the ground was the incessant rumbling of tyres. Ahead of us an arrow-straight, man made, strip of tarmac thickened out towards us from the base of distant, dead hills. A pure canvas domed above, a rainbow of blues, as if we were riding off into the sunset in a Hollywood movie. Off to our left a slovenly section of sky had fallen with a splosh onto the land. The lake appeared to be a wide hole passing directly through Earth, yet its location was all wrong, what was it doing there? This was desert, cracked rock, treeless, nothing alive. We wanted to get to it, to prove it was there, but our map showed a white road, a rough piste, and our nerve failed us.

Source bleu de Meski, a romantic-sounding spot, was our target resting place for the night. Chris and Tina had stopped there, now just a few days ahead of us, and relayed the news that Mohammed was waiting for us. They told us they'd had a riotous good time there, from our experiences of travelling with them, fabulous companions throughout the seas, trees, mountains and cities of Northern Spain and Portugal, we could only guess what might have occurred.

Our entrance into the camping area was delayed a little, as we drove straight past the sign for it, perhaps with too much momentum from hours of concentration. On our second pass, our confidence of being on target was low. Along the road an unwelcoming wall of mud houses sat opposite a flattened pile of rubbish, light blue and orange plastic bags were held captive in the breeze by whatever waste they held within. Two donkeys in convoy ahead of us slowed to a halt, carefully moving forwards, stepping over something in their path. A trench ran across the road, cut square. Looking at it we were unsure of its depth, mental images of wheel-cracking, axle-snapping carnage stopped us from going any further. We waited as an oncoming car approached, only for it drive straight across, no hesitation. Once it passed we did the same, with a *thdum-thdum*.

A man approached us, a white man, with an easy, relaxed gait. He was a French restaurant owner he said, opportunely handing over a business card, its smooth surface and clean letters felt alien in the surroundings. Pointing to a concrete square forming a corner of the town, itself a square shape, he offered, *"come and order what you want two hours before, so we can cook it for you"*. A steep, high sided ramp lead us quickly, unnervingly, down from the desert. Levelling out, palm trees towered above, casting long-fingered shadows. From amidst the endless dust and dry rock above, we found ourselves lowered into a cool oasis, a channel of water to our right chasing past us into the camp.

The camp entrance routine varies from place to place, most employ a fairly hands-off approach with their guests, taking details and sometimes nominating a place to park. Mohammed had other ideas, we were about to be efficiently processed! In a light brown robe, youthful smooth skin and a thoughtful, genuine ambience, he jumped from his seat at the entrance and lifted a barrier. He caught us by surprise, camouflaged along with more elderly but no less observant compatriots, against a wall of hanging robes, pots and paintings. Above the entrance a sign read: *Depot Berbere*, the Berbers making up a good percentage of the Moroccan ethnic mix alongside Arabs. Catching our attention again Mohammed waved us through, lowered the barrier and motioned for us to follow him. Negotiating wide palm trunks, their heights invisible without craning our necks, he indicated a place to park, soft dust billowing beneath his feet appearing as though Dave was taking up a position on the moon.

Mohammed shook our hands, easy going, with deep brown eyes and an ounce of insecurity, he was entirely disarming. We felt like his first ever guests. He was expecting us, *"Yes, yes, Chris told me you were coming, and to look after you, welcome, welcome"*. Another robed man turned up, carrying a roll over his shoulder. Placing it next to our door, he carefully rolled out the red mat before walking away, a single nod acknowledging us. Mohammed explained it was to keep the sand out of our van, it worked perfectly. We took a few steps on it, enjoying the feeling of this little luxury.

With an *"I show you around"*, Mohammed set off around the site, walking slightly ahead and turning periodically to check we were following. Pointing at the normally decrepit toilet block, we noticed a wooden plaque with a drawn-on silhouette of an ancient camcorder, with a red circle and slashed line, the universal 'not allowed' symbol. No video recording in the toilets? We still can't imagine what must have happened to have made such a sign necessary. A metal staircase clung onto the side of the toilet block. Jay made a quick dash up it after the tour for a view, flinching and quickly descending again as a man awoke from his afternoon sleep, lifting his head from a corner of the roof.

After a proud indication of water tap location, Mohammed led us on to the climax, the Source Bleu. *"Sacred fish, but you can swim with them"* he tells us, waving his hand over a rectangular swimming pool, loaded with small black fish, the walls and floor clumped with patches of something organic. The water was cold, too cold to swim in we said, glad of the excuse. A few other motorhomes sat to one side of the camp, but none of the other guests were accompanying the fish either. Seeing us testing the water, Mohammed told us it comes from the ground. Several springs breached the ground here, slicing out the vast crack in the earth we were stood in. The pool and others were fashioned by French Legionnaires, no doubt a welcome relief during oven-hot summers.

The Source Bleu spring runs through the mountain above and exits the bedrock in a shaded alcove carved out in the vertical sides of the desert crack. We walked over a tiny bridge from the swimming pool and looked down into the beautifully clear spring water, a deep shade of blue green. Mohammed told us a quick story about a nomadic tribe, who normally travelled at night to avoid the heat. One day a member of the tribe came here in the light of the day and, leaning over the pool, saw his vivid blue head wrap reflected in the water. Making the assumption the water itself gave off the colour, the source received its name: the Blue Spring of the town of Meski.

Within the bare confines of Mohammed's office back at the site entrance, he looked crestfallen when told we were only staying one night. Chris and Tina had been in touch, they were at Erg Chebbi on the edge of the Sahara. Only a few hour's drive south, we were keen to finally catch them up. His smile soon crept back and walking outside we heard a call *"Abdul!"*. A boy appeared, legs stretched on an oversized brake-less mountain bike. Dropping it on the floor, he stood hands on hips, next to Mohammed, who advised this was his little brother. In a light brown jacket and turned up jeans, Abdul would blend in in most European cities. Perhaps eight or ten years old, dark skin to match his brother and with short-cropped black hair, we guessed Abdul was being trained to deal with tourists: *"Abdul will take you to old kasbah"*.

We fetched Charlie, who needed a walk after long hours in the van, Abdul remained unfazed, the picture of cool, serious and world-wise for his age. He walked off in the direction of the camp entrance. Flip flops slapping against his socked feet, we sensed he was a tiny bit confused about his lumbering, curious charges. Following the river, he would point out something here and there, speaking French, normally nothing more than a single word. Walking past women bent over washing clothes in the river, they looked up at us and our furry creature on-a-rope. Chris and Tina had taken the same trip a few days before, and at this point their dog Loli had chosen to go to the loo. Chris had used a plastic bag to retrieve it, in the accepted European fashion, causing the ladies in the river to retch.

On a one-person wide packed mud path beneath palms, Abdul pointed at patches of cultivated land. Onions, coriander, olives, oranges, potatoes and other crops we couldn't between us work out the name of. Along with the palm dates, everything Meski needed to eat could be grown here, and more besides. Along the edge of each plot a small trench, some still drying from their last use, gave away age-old irrigation methods. Small wooden boards guided the flow of spring water here and there. To cross the spring, two palms had been dropped side by side, one bending lower than the other. Charlie, sensing twin fears of height and water, flattened himself against the dirt, before inevitably being scraped up by Jay and the two teetered across the makeshift bridge, facing upstream. Abdul held Julie's hand, a young gentleman, edging himself along in front.

On the other side, above a climb of almost-natural steps, stood the kasbah. An entire wrecked, abandoned town. The smooth walls of mud-encased stones snapped like a biscuit, still guarding the edge of the chasm it perched on. The oasis below was a river of green, the tree tops reached to just below the level of the desert floor, smoothing off the plain with bushy green palms. Standing on stones released from the kasbah, the sight across the plain took hold of us, we stared. The cool and calm air killed any noise from below, Abdul stood patiently, leaning against the kasbah in the shade. Within a few minutes Charlie indicated it was time to continue, cracking open the silence with scrabbling claws and a whine of boredom.

Abdul moved easily through the roofless space of the old town. He would walk along in an effortless dance across the fallen rocks from the walls around us. Our progress was slower. Our eyes flickered between the floor, doorways and the pale blue sky glinting through windowless stone frames and the openness above us. The main street of the old town, wide enough for a cart, called for care, the walls appeared in the very act of tumbling inwards. Off to each side, small rooms marked out where shops had been. Although little more than a corner or an archway, our imaginations were supported by the present day visions we'd seen in Chefchaouen and Fes, our minds placed animated sellers into their doorways.

Throughout the town the walls were rough, stone innards revealed by the wind like stacked teeth. The only place wrapped in smooth render, as an indication of civilisation which lived here, was the mosque. Hesitating at the door, unsure of etiquette, Abdul waved us in. Archways towered above us, unlikely survivors of the passing of time. The lower section of the broad square minaret, long silent, stood like the proud stump of a generations-old oak, its roots buried deep in the kasbah floor. Abdul stood alongside a well, its dark innards still descending the 20 metres to the spring below. Water was needed for washing before and after prayers.

Making our way out into the remainder of the town, the walls dropped low. In gaps the plain and hazy brown mountains seemed to quietly whisper: *we were here before, watching, and will be here long after this is all dust.* Alone, but for our child guide, within the skeleton of the old town, we shivered. Not for fear of robed ghosts, but for the present physical lack of sunlight within the shadows. As the fortunes of local leaders had waned, and funds for continual repairs to the walls became elusive, the natural collapse had started. This in turn urged the townsfolk out and over the oasis, the seed of the present day town was planted. The mud-covered walls look the same, but now they cloak enduring concrete, encasing reinforcing metal bars, progress. At a back entrance to the kasbah, Abdul stepped out onto the sunlit two-dimensional rock of the plain, we followed, and we stared. Beyond the unnatural vertical of the walls nothing dared break the unrelenting horizontal of the desert, tumbling colour-matched brush a foot tall the only exception. Looking to the south the vista was equally split by a ruler-straight line, blue sky cut cleanly by featureless dry earth. Abdul posed with Julie against this backdrop, his thumb tucked easily into a rear pocket, smiling, uncertain why anyone would be interested in all this crumbling nothingness.

Having patiently granted us long minutes of silent staring, Abdul started back towards the camp, taking a rock-strewn path along a dry river bed in the shadow of the kasbah. In the patch of land to his right many of the larger stones stood upright. Abdul explained they were headstones. Wordless, unmade and unattached to the earth but by their own weight, they seemed a perfect way to mark a resting place here.

Mohammed was waiting for us as we returned to the camp, inviting us into the *Depot Berbere* for a welcoming mint tea, which we took to mean there was business to be done. Still looking for blankets, this could be an opportunity for us to get them, but we had to put Mohammed off for a few minute's breathing space. Before entering the shop, a search around Dave's cupboards turned out a small solar-powered torch, coloured pencils and a handful of sweets. Looking at it on the table, we questioned ourselves, *was this enough for a two hour tour?* Abdul seemed to think so, gracefully accepting when we called him over and explained the torch, he'd not seemed to be expecting anything at all. A friend of his spied the transaction and tried his luck, asking for sweets. The poor young man was rewarded with a lecture in broken French about reward being given for a service, and slunk off sweetless.

Remembering the need to pre-order our food, we made our way up the steep ramp from the camp and stepped over the small trench which ran the full length of the road. The restaurant proved easy to locate, but difficult to believe it was the right place. Devoid of signs, we found ourselves building up courage to open a plain metal doorway into someone's house. Entering a tiny courtyard, steps to the right led up to the flat roof, a door stood ajar to our left, we leaned around it. Inside three tables stood in the company of a large TV and a stereo. This was the place, although it was clear it was the French couple's living space as well as their business. The Frenchman appeared in response to a knock, and we ordered our meals from a short list, Julie chose an omelette and was shown a jar of dried porcini mushrooms, asking if they would be acceptable as they didn't have any fresh. With a time agreed to return, the *depot* called.

Mohammed sat us on short stools against a low round table inside the shop. A cold place, the shelved walls overflowed with items which we glanced at in moments of silence. Abdul brought a tray, a silver pot with a swan neck steamed, surrounded by decorated shot-glasses. There was no fresh mint here, the tea came straight from the pot, poured into a glass before being poured back into the pot, all part of the ritual. *"Berber whiskey!"* Mohammed announced, explaining this non-alcoholic stuff was enough for him, although some *modern Berbers* drank alcohol. Islamic law forbids intoxicating substances, as it does pre-marital sex. As we'd already found out for ourselves, not every Muslim in Morocco abstains from alcohol, and for non-Muslim foreigners like us, the laws appear to be overlooked.

Once he judged the tea was ready, Mohammed poured it into the small glasses from a height, important to build up some froth. Making small talk and cupping the glass for warmth, Mohammed answered our questions. Yes, he went on holiday, Essaouira was his favourite place, a resort town on the Atlantic coast. The people he met had taught him English, slowly, along with several other languages, all a part of being in the tourist trade here. He was also a musician, playing the drums for tourists in Marrakech during the summer.

As the tea ran dry, so did conversation. We asked Mohammed if we could look around the rest of the shop. *"Yes, yes, of course, come inside".* The rear room was larger, and equally packed with all things Berber, bright rough-piled rugs, striped blue and beige bobbly jackets, a four-stringed instrument of some kind, crude metal jewellery on leather bands, everywhere something unusual to us. In an effort to retain some bargaining power, we pretended to ignore the blankets. Nothing, of course, was labelled with a price.

"Idriss is coming!, Idriss is coming!". Jumping sideways at Mohammed's excited announcement, we gathered his uncle was on his way, the shop owner. Ah,

it became clear, Mohammed was merely the warm-up act, Idriss was the deal-closer. We stopped looking at the shelves, fascination and trepidation turned our heads towards the doorway. Voices outside announced his arrival before his round figure filled the entrance and burst through it. He beamed, holding out his hand to us in turn, speaking English. Wildly cross-eyed, perhaps blind in one of them, dressed in a vivid blue robe with swinging necklaces, Idriss' appearance sparked off a small explosion of activity.

After telling us what kind and wonderful people our friends were, he moved around the room taking up this and that and showing it to us. With no pause in movement, no gap in speech, we flowed along in his wake. Fending off the rugs, we explained our camping car was too small for them. *"You're a good fatima!"* Idriss smiled at Julie when she explained she only wore earrings from her wedding day. Repeated parries around the shop eventually exhausted Idriss *"Is there anything you want to buy?"*. Julie pointed at the Berber blankets, Idriss walked to them, and the bargaining began. *"We no rush, not like George Bush!"* Mohammed smiled, appearing from the shadows, we smiled back, bemused.

The purpose of the advance drinking of tea, it seems, is to enable parties to assess each other and to fortify them. An hour passed, frenetic with activity, before we sat down in Dave, opened out two folded blankets and smiled. Electronics are a valuable commodity in Morocco, and the bargaining started not with a money value, but with a request: *"Do you have any phones, laptops?"* we had neither spare, but working our way around the van we surprised ourselves at what we did have and didn't need. USB memory sticks, more solar torches, a wind-up radio (which Idriss failed to get a station on but accepted anyway), some earphones. *"Trousers, shoes?"* Julie headed back into the van while Idriss, seeing a redundant Jay looking at the instrument on the wall, offered to play it. Taking it down, he slowly sat down and placed his fingers into the fret-less stick jutting from the round body of the thing. The noise was awful. When Julie re-appeared smiles cracked our faces as he finally gave in torturing the thing and eyed up a pair of walking trousers which no longer fitted Julie. The deal was eventually done, after much gesturing, mock-serious much of the time, for a sum of money and the inevitable inclusion of a few bricks of wine.

As Julie and Idriss shook hands, the hand drums came out from under a shelf. This time the lightning fast blur of Mohammed and Idriss' hands over the tight surfaces was enchanting, fingers and palms hammering away, encouraging our feet to dance about as we sat. Drumming for an age, the entrance of a number of other people into the room including a young girl who photographed the group, had us questioning: *"is this the announcement to the town that some more suckers have been ripped off and there are second hand electronics for sale?"*. It wasn't. A group of friends had arrived who hadn't been seen for a long time, we smiled and with a few *bonjours* backed out of the shop, as they laughed and talked together, drums finally silent.

After a couple of minutes in Dave to catch our breath, 7:30pm rolled around, time to eat. Within the tiny multi-use restaurant, two of the tables had been pushed together, a group of French people relaxed around them. Acknowledging us as we sat to one side, we could immediately sense their innate enjoyment of the ritual as ingredients were brought for them to inspect and nod over. As knives and bread were delivered, we asked our hosts' names: *Alain,* while *Denise* remained unseen in the kitchen. The night cool has been in some way warmed in the small room and we removed our coats, enjoying the magnificently flavoured food, quickly delivered as we were a few minutes late.

In between courses as we waited for liquor-fired orange slices, we asked Alain about the trench. *"Ah, Ca, c'est l'internet",* we understood, the world wide web and email was arriving down a cable to this dusty corner of the desert. We hoped it was already here though, travelling in its wireless form, as we wanted to fulfil our commitment to update our internet diary every day. We'd been unable to get any signal in the deep crack in the desert that houses the oasis, so we took our kit with us to the restaurant on the desert surface. Alain pointed skywards, we'd get a signal on the roof. Sure enough we did, tapping out typo-filled gibberish and uploading our eager photos of this other-world in the dark. Returning inside, our French co-eaters pulled out laptops as they learned of the signal from above.

We should have been shattered, but our blood pulsed. Mohammed collected the money and wine for the blankets in the dark, a practised fluid motion saw it disappear under his robe: *"What Allah does not see".* With this final task complete, Julie captured the magnificence of the stars, shadowed by palm leaves, with a seconds-long shutter speed on her camera before we both finally collapsed, pulling one of the blankets over us, Charlie's grunting snores lulling us to sleep.

The following day, restless and eager to see more of the new town above, Jay walked up the slope out of the campsite, leaving, a reluctant to move, Charlie to keep, an equally reluctant to move, Julie company. Alone, the silent mud grid of the town was intimidating. The learned trick of the stick pick-up saw off a pack of roaming dogs, their thin bodies ungainly prancing away over the mud and rubbish above the oasis. Black, scraggy goats a distance away were herded, with a waved stick, by an elderly moustached man in a faded red baseball cap, one hand tucked in a pocket. He kicked at the plastic bags strewn around with the side of his foot, using the stick to turn over items of interest. Looking as though he was seriously considering picking up and eating an old bit of orange Jay walked over to him, and placed a few Dirhams into his calloused hands, drawing a few-toothed smile and a *"merci, merci"*.

Building small courage, Jay entered the unsealed outer streets of the new town. Shadow cast across all but the widest of thoroughfares, the streets were cold, silent. A donkey standing tethered at the ankle and the distant back of a figure offered no company. Doorways and windows stared, featureless metal and wooden doors and shutters blanking them off. Around a corner Jay met the goats again, their heads held low over the grass-less dust. Not wanting to offend, Jay gestured to the herder with the camera, he was greeted with a cheery acceptance. In the photograph the goats stand to the foreground, in the shadow of a wall chalked with Arabic above the numbered squares of an election campaign. The man smiles, walking with the empty no-man's land behind.

A man cycling through the town on a tired, old bicycle interrupted his ride to open his nearby, bedraggled shop for a single foreigner. Inside was full of dusty boxes, but the produce was fresh, so his opportunism was rewarded. Julie was greeted with gathered goods: oranges, green peppers, a cucumber and onions from the shop, a huge round of fresh bread wrapped in a striped tea-towel from Mohammed, given for free. Was the price paid at the shop fair? We had no idea.

The last stage of the 850km trek south to catch up with Tina and Chris awaited. Mohammed saw us preparing to leave and walked over, handing us a scrap of paper with the name of the kasbah he'd recommended to our friends. In the spirit of things in this little oasis, rather than giving a tip, we chose something from among our things to give to Mohammed as a thank you for taking care of us: a furry hot water bottle to keep him warm on the cold winter nights. We had to explain how it worked. He smiled and held it a little away from himself, as though fearing that it might bite him.

The fury gift was soon forgotten when Mohammed's attention was caught by our mountain bikes, long unused and dirty from the road, locked to Dave's rack. He walked around, taking in what we thought to be the poor state of the bikes, instead surprising us with a statement of their high worth, breaking the golden rule of haggling. Now we had the upper-hand, the sought after goods, Mohammed was going to face a tougher haggle than he had bargained for. It wasn't a difficult decision to get rid of Julie's bike, she never got on with it, so it had barely been used so far on the trip. Also locked to the bike rack was a thing of glowing hate for Charlie: a child's chariot. We'd bought it with the hope we could tow him along as we cycled into towns, in reality every time we used it he whined and tried to leap out.

We hooked up the chariot to the bike and smiled as Abdul provided a thorough demonstration circling the palm trees, the rolled rug from by Dave's door sticking out of the chariot at an angle. The announced monetary value of the bike didn't translate to actual money in the hand of course, Julie drove a hard bargain and we left with a huge silk throw and a Berber-style wool jacket for Jay, we also threw in the free bottle of sidra we had been given with our ferry tickets.

The bike leant against a palm tree by the entrance alongside other bikes, the chances of it actually propelling Abdul to school, as promised, seemed rather low, but we didn't mind, it would be much more useful here. To prolong its life, a pump, lock, inner tube, water bottle and puncture repair kit were thrown into the bargain after the deal was already done. The final gesture of kindness came from Mohammed. As we drove past the shop he ran out to us, and through Dave's side window passed two items to Julie. The first was a Berber compass, the metal star-shaped pendant grasping a rounded, coloured stone. From Idriss' sales pitch last night we knew they were for navigating by the stars, Mohammed told us we could use it to return there one day soon. The other item was a sticker for Dave. We thanked him for everything and headed up the slope back onto the crusted earth of the desert, away from the small, strange world and the lives being lived in the crack of an oasis.

As we got back onto the main road south we looked at the sticker and smiled: the Moroccan wrapped star under the word *Maroc*, sat above a yellow circle of stars on a blue background. Morocco made a bid to join the EU in 1987 and was officially turned down on the rather easy excuse of geography - Morocco not actually being in Europe, the reasons were far more likely to do with distance from democracy and human rights standards than from Brussels.

A DUNE REUNION

The road south was a good quality sealed road, a nice, bright, red line on our map. For the last few paper centimetres it was a white line, stretching to the town of Merzouga. We were heading just north of the town and looking at the map, this was a very good thing. South of Merzouga the white line became dotted, a piste road - an unknown entity. A few small town names appear along it, then nothing. Even the dotted piste trails dry up, leaving small blue and white circles marking out water holes in the desert. The next road to the south is in Algeria, but the border isn't marked on our map. Perhaps because there is no point claiming ownership of dust, or maybe it's because the border has been closed for years in a spat over Morocco's disputed occupation of the Western Sahara region.

Moving along the red section of road, the views coming through Dave's windows were of pink earth and cubed mud houses, groups of palm trees would flourish below the level of the road, each an explosion of muted green frozen in time. Between the trees smoke puffed up and thinned out, obscuring sections of the plateaued land around each lengthy oasis. Human sights captured our attention. A group of boys, Abdul's age and wearing the same western garb, leaning on a single bike and smiling. Men in mismatched boiler suits stood under three tall poles spiked into a teepee, the line of rope suspended from it penetrating the earth below them. A dark, skinny donkey, its back shielded by a cloth from the rubbing load of white sacks it carried. A blue robed man asleep in a dirty white plastic chair. Two women, heavily wrapped in blankets, heads leaned in towards one another talking, the small head of a boy peering sideways at us from his swaddling on one of their backs. We, or more accurately Dave, was smiled and waved at ceaselessly. From opportunist nippers, trained by preceding travellers to ask for something for free, to the man, slowly riding a red tractor with a white, plastic roof and a tiny windscreen, thanking us for our patience as we carefully overtook him.

The land we were travelling through was as poor in money as it is in rain, yet it seemed to exist, if not prosper, with neither. Some people worked, easily visible, hack-sawing a metal door frame in the street, carrying loads on animals or on an increasing number of bicycles. Many others did nothing but squat in the sun, alone or in small groups, and watch the world go by them. The people in this remote land seem content with the status-quo. Change, seen as an absolute foundation of life in the west, to them must be an alien and simply unnecessary concept.

Clusters of sellers appeared along the route, all selling the same thing, mostly using the same technique, thrusting a handful of the stuff they're selling into the road as you drive past. The commodity changes depending on where you are in the country; honey, dates, rose oil, argan oil, dyed crystals, whatever is to hand. Many place their goods in an elevated position and retire to the shade, leaving a ghostly line of used plastic bottles, no indication of their contents, sitting on stones or hanging from trees by the roadside. Fossils filled the lay-bys here, wooden trellises packed with grey, polished shapes, leggy trilobites, helter-skelter ammonites and smooth cone orthoceras. Our guide book advised us many were fakes, too perfect. A diplodocus skeleton strode out, an eyeless head turned towards the road, white letters on the building behind advertised a MUSEAM FOSSIL AND MINERAL. We laughed, cynically perhaps, knowing that the museum sold everything inside. Skeletons of the competing museums froze as we drove past, pointing them out to each other, the ferociously dead T-Rex winning our in-cab competition.

The N13, the white road, and gateway to Erg Chebbi, sprouts out from a kink in the road at Rissani. An enormous archway, topped off with five red flags and straddled by man-sized arches, announces the town, no need for a nameplate. The main arch, tall enough for a lorry, squeezes traffic to single file but causes no inconvenience; there were few motorized vehicles here. Rissani bustled, thick with people. Metal doored and sign-less shops stood closed, seemingly abandoned. The smooth painted metal, used only for industrial purposes in the west, was used here from necessity, there are so few trees. Among the open shops, universally announced by a stack of coca-cola crates, others were more warmly closed, their entrances covered with a hanging striped blanket or crossed by a propped broom handle. Towns here were purely functional affairs, the larger ones always preceded with a road block. An increasing number of women chose to cover their faces with a scarf, something we'd hardly seen further north and outside tiny shops, deep blue Tuareg head scarves flutter in the breeze - we were getting very close to the desert.

Searching for the sign to Merzouga, ever-helpful Shat-nav showing the tarmac we were driving along as open desert, so we slowed at a junction. A man leapt from the side of the street, desperate to grab our attention. The words of our guidebook echoed in our ears, *the town is famous for touts,* we kept moving. With no further clues to tell us if we were on the right road we had little choice but to carry on. The buildings beside the road thinned out and soon the sheer vastness of the desert confirmed we were heading in the right direction.

The desert of our imaginations was a sandy place, blown around into vast dunes, the odd palm tree. The desert in this reality was an astoundingly empty plain of scattered rocks and talcum-dust. Any breakdown of our trusty, if long-in-the-tooth vehicle in Europe is efficiently handled by a German corporation, a yellow recovery truck appearing over the horizon, lights spinning, within an hour or so. Here, such an organised group was laughable, we were on our own. Nowhere did we feel it more than on this lonely stretch of rough tarmac running headlong into the desert, only the impending meeting with friends would remove the worry entirely.

Travelling onwards towards the shimmering southern horizon, an inviting warm sea of stones, we searched on our left for the erg, the dunes, and the reason this road existed - to bring tourists. In the vast Saharan scale of things, Erg Chebbi is merely an elongated eye drop of yellow on the map. At only 22 kilometres north to south, and ten kilometres at its widest, the sands are washed around by the wind. Growing dunes of up to 150 metres tall, yet, for some unfathomable reason, never shifting far from their roots, the pure orange sands were the desert of our imaginations. Before we could see the dunes, miles-long piste tracks started to sprout from the tarmac road. Running away at right angles, each turning was signalled by a fistful of signs: *Auberge Berbers, L'Etoile Des Dunes, Auberge Kasbah Leile,* this last one etched in white on a camel-shaped sign. They guided tourists to the strip of hotels, calling themselves *kasbahs, riads* and *auberges,* along the Western edge of the dune. We stared along them, eyeing the broken surface, mindful of a snapped suspension spring.

The erg appeared. A thin line of creamy pale orange, like a distant mountain range, splitting the black dirt of the desert and the lightening sky as it sank to the ground. The road continued, more thickets of signs, then a bright blue polished oddity waited alongside the road, an Afriqua fuel station, perhaps it was lost? We'd filled up earlier expecting to see no diesel along this finger of a road, poking into the unknown. Searching the signs for the name Mohammed had carefully written on a scrap of paper in wobbly upper case letters, we finally found it. *KASBAH TOMBOUCTOU*, white on a navy blue rectangle, an unnecessary arrow pointing along the eastern-running dirt.

Dropping off the road, we started along the piste, a brushed dirt road, the largest of the rocks ushered to the side. In the distance, a cloud of dust chased a black square towards us. Dave pushed on at a crawl, the undulations of the piste causing cupboard contents to bounce on their shelves. The square became a Mitsubishi four by four, aiming for us on the single track. We stopped as we closed in, it carried on without pause, diving off the track a way in front of us, ploughing past in an even greater cloud, before dodging back onto the piste in our rear-view mirrors. We were glad we'd had the foresight to close Dave's windows from the ensuing dust storm.

As we edged closer the dunes grew from adolescent mounds to fully fledged butter-sculpted, magnificent heights. At their feet, tiny palms and walls marked out the line of hospitality, signalling that the dunes might change shape, but never moved home. Our dirt track ran to a set of walls, two miniature camels stood nose to nose forming an archway where they met. The camels grew, until they towered over us and Dave made his way underneath their necks. A palm-lined drive lead to a group of turrets, wrapped with a hatched pattern they merged with tall walls to form a palace. An entrance archway, double the height of a man with a red carpet lolled out like a tongue, mouthed at us: *are you sure you're in the right place?* We really weren't too sure as our friends and their gleaming grey motorhome were nowhere to be seen.

The reception was dark after the glare of the desert sun. As our eyes became accustomed we could make out an opulent cool and airy place, opening out to the rear, but still with no sign of Tina and Chris. Empty, patterned sofas awaited guests, the huge mirrors reflecting only us. Only our hands ran over the smooth, polished marble fossil shapes, clumped together and stood in relief on a thigh-high stab of stone. At the reception desk, a sharp-uniformed man greeted our questions about camping cars with confusion. We retrieved Mohammed's scrap of paper, next to the name of the kasbah was another word Hamid. It switched on a light, *"Ah, vous devez parler avec Hamid"*, and Hamid was called for on the telephone.

Hamid, we soon found, knew something about tourism. His figure was a head-to-toe perfected image of the desert, a nomad, his light robe flowed as he walked, his head wrapped in a Tuareg scarf, feet slapped in sandals. He spoke good English, but was careful with his words. Communicating with slight mannerisms, a wave of the hand and a nod of the head, he told us we were in the right place. *Follow-me*, a slow sideways nod of the head requested. Stepping out onto a stone-paved terrace, Hamid's hand waved us into seats around a metal table, a waiter was instantly by his side and mint tea was ordered, Hamid was clearly in an elevated position around here.

The rear of the kasbah opened immediately out onto the dunes. Palms looked in-place here, despite being clearly placed at the whim of man. A group of camels stood, kneeled and lay. A grey motorhome glinted in the sun. Our hearts jumped, it was Christina, Chris and Tina's adventure wagon. Making our apologies to Hamid, who was unfazed, we ran over to our friends, who were sat in their camping chairs, reading books and soaking up sun in this unlikely paradise. Hugs and smiles! We'd first met over a very, late autumn night of wow-cheap *Rioja* and *pintxos* in cosy San Sebastian bars. Our friendship was forged driving the Picos de Europa mountains and the harbours and bays of Northern Spain and Portugal. We hadn't seen them since sharing Christmas near Lisbon, after which they'd embarked on an epic drive to Spain to meet family for New Year's Eve. On this remote stage set at the farthest reach of our comfort zone, the rendez-vous was doubly sweet, we hugged again and babbled.

Hamid sat still and silently called, his lack of words creating a strange tension after the machine-gun patter of his compatriots in the north, the mint tea had arrived. Pouring it out, back in, and out again, Hamid repeated a now familiar pattern, before pouring high, and being rewarded with a good froth. We asked where he was from. *"Merzouga"*, he gestured south. In between staring off in thought, Hamid told us he could organise trips. Camels, four by four, quad bikes, we could talk about it later. We nodded. Lost in awe and searching for sensible conversation we told him how beautiful we found the kasbah and the dunes. Hamid considered this, as though it were some revelation. *"Yes they are beautiful"*, he finally said, *"they are the largest dunes in Morocco, maybe even the world"*.

We drank quickly, eager to allow Charlie to meet Loli again. Hamid didn't seem to sense this, there was no urgency in him, no need to move or speak, whatever needed him would come to him. Eventually he stood and told us he would show us around. We followed him along roped paths between palms to a bar lined with familiar bottles. An outdoor pool, being cleaned despite being spotless, was chilly to the touch, welcome in summer, but this was the start of February and we wore jeans and fleeces. Through a broad wooden door, the spa area, showers and toilets we could use, a hammam, massage rooms, a relaxation room and a jacuzzi. This was our kind of campsite. We didn't discuss the price to stay, but Chris had already told us that it was half the cost of the sites in the north. Hamid left us at reception, *if you need anything, just ask for me.*

Smiling, we skipped over the ground to Dave, and drove him around to where Christina was parked among a few palm trees between the Kasbah and the dunes. Plugging the power cable into a socket in one of the palm trees, we released Charlie to sniff up sand while we sat in the sun in our camping chairs and caught up with Chris and Tina, laughing at the luxury. The kasbah was a place for celebrities, Shakira as well as Hillary and Chelsea Clinton had stopped here. But in the winter sun, it was quite empty, the odd coach load of Japanese tourists would arrive, take a camel trip, stop for the night and leave. Apart from the staff, who roamed the grounds in green-blue robes for uniforms, and men tending the camels, we had the place, and its facilities to ourselves.

Chris and Tina are unified with boundless energy. They'd managed to stay the desire to climb the highest peak of sand, until we had arrived. They had used their time to trek across the sands mounted on swing-gaited camels, their backsides and thighs sore from hours of gripping. With the distance to the summit hard to judge, the six of us set off at 3pm. Rucksacks loaded with water, cameras, a plastic sheet and chocolate, we walked straight towards the orange dunes. A *sandstorm could lose a man within a hundred meters of camp*, a disembodied voice had warned over the internet. Looking around the air was calm, palm leaves hung heavy and lazy. Passing the herd of idling camels waiting for the next tourist bottom to be taken for a trek, Tina remarked that this was the first place in the world she'd been lulled to sleep by indolent camel snorts.

The dunes changed, not only with the wind, but with the hour, colour-shifting through an orange-gold down towards deeper reds as the sun set. We found the sand could be hard and therefore easy to traverse, or soft and grabbing. The soft challenged us, particularly Charlie with his short legs. His face registered genuine concern when he was buried up to his belly. We learned quickly how to avoid the softest patches, choosing paths across rounded peaks. This cooling February afternoon we saw few footsteps in the sand, our nearest neighbours upright ants on a distant dune. It was hard to imagine the crowded mayhem of peak season that we'd read about, the wealthy four by four engined crowds at play.

Our target dune walked towards us, closer and steeper than we imagined. Loli eased her way past the group, at a distinct advantage as the rest of us were now also on all fours. Charlie required rescue, carrying up the steepest section and dropped onto a ridge towards the top. Topping out on our mini-clamber, we expected the sun to be dipping close to the horizon, instead it stood high in the sky, we'd only walked a few hundred meters. We sat in the sand on top of the dune sipping water, talking for hours about the trips we'd taken, people we'd met, where we might go next. This was an entirely different Morocco, pure opulence and natural beauty. The call to prayer from a distant minaret echoed quietly, tapping us, reminding us where we were.

We'd taken a plastic sheet with the manly hope of being able to launch ourselves, with a whoop, down the slope. Unlike the compacted, mud-snow park slopes of our childhoods, the sand here sank, and so did we. Not even a helpful push would gain momentum. Deprived of whooshing speed, we chose the next best option - the roll. Weeks later rivulets of sand would still be seeping out of pockets and shoes. A light breeze halted play, sand whipping up and stinging our faces. Hoods up and scarves on we turned our backs to it. Relief came as the wind quickly eased, yet its short existence was enough to load the mechanism of our cameras with grinding Saharan grains, causing us to wince as we tried to capture the sunset. A bath of cloud soaked up the sun as it sank below the horizon. We didn't care, we were exhilarated.

Tina and Chris had whetted our appetites for dinner. Somehow, treated as equals to the high paying oriental guests, we could eat at the auberge buffet. The price? Less than we paid in the faux-Chefchaouen restaurant. The food was beautifully presented and there was plenty of it. With a cheeky beer dripping cool condensation on the table, we should have felt guilt, but it didn't come. We ate and drank heartily, accompanied by a long table of chatting Japanese guests, the camel meat a favourite, more for novelty than chewy texture. Stomachs packed, we headed to the spa and booked into the *hammam* for the following morning in an effort to de-sand ourselves. None of us knew quite what a hammam was, our Fes guide had briefly explained Moroccans use them in place of showers or baths at home, somewhere to get clean and meet friends. In the evening the air cooled, sitting in Dave our electrical heater stopping the chill, we chatted over a box or two of Spanish wine, planning the coming days.

LOBSTERS AND CAMPERS IN THE DESERT

Tina had infected Julie with a previously unknown desire to see the sun rise above the erg. At 5:30am, attempts to infuse Jay with the same wish failed, so Julie took up a sentinel position outside, a coat and Berber blanket shielding her from the cold night air, and the world from her pyjamas. The stars above faded slowly from sight as the unseen sun rounded the Earth dissolving the black sky into an inky blue. The camels grunted at the dawning day. Jay too grunted, pulling a chair alongside Julie and bringing a welcome duvet. The camel men had already begun their day, silhouettes passing across the smoke-free fire in front of their square tent. Either through awareness of their awakened keepers or through an innate enlivening with the coming sun, the camels themselves arose, standing and snorting. Birds tweeted, fleeting between palms, dodging shadows. The sky paled in fear of its glowing master. An edge of bright white announced the sun, firing the sharp curve of a dune. We clasped hands, and shielded our eyes. With the sun fully rounded, we carried our chairs and coverings back, watched by the camel men sat hunched over their fire. They must bear witness to this magnificence every day of their lives.

At 7am still wide awake we added to our sense of Dali surrealism, using our internet connection to listen to a British radio station. Chris Evans' laughing voice reminded us of traffic jams, dark drives to work, dark drives home and our friends. We listened and smiled, looking at the dunes yellowing through the window.

Our allotted hammam time arrived. We stood ready and waiting, beside the empty swimming pool, staring at a locked door. We consulted the pool cleaning man. The hammam was closed and it would take until 1pm to warm it up. Not collectively convinced he was an authority on all things hammam, we sought a second opinion at reception. The hammam was already heating and would be ready in ten minutes. We walked back round to the pool and relaxed on the loungers in the morning sunshine. We were just too punctual for Morocco.

In the hammam, a middle-aged lady in a pure white dress guided us into the first room. Deep blue tiles ran along the floor and arched over us, giving it a cosy, warm feeling. Sitting on a bench, waiting for each of us, was a basket with a towelling robe, rough black *kessel* mitten, for sloughing off dead skin, and flip flops. We looked around for private changing and realised we were in it. Stood in front of our friends, prudishness persisted in the form of eyes glued to the wall as we changed. Normally men and women use the Hammam separately, either at different times or in different rooms, wearing dark underwear. But this wasn't your normal Hammam, it was a five star spa Hammam, so we were allowed to go in together and all opted for swimwear, over which we donned our bathrobes and waited to be told what to do.

A young girl entered the room, closing the door behind her she pointed at our robes, they were for afterwards. We placed them back into the baskets and followed. She took us quickly through a second, tiled and curved roofed-room and into a third, the heat building between rooms. Both of these two rooms had a tiled sink, overflowing with water, alongside which sat thick leather buckets. The third room had a wide table in the middle. We laughed as we sat on the heated, tiled bench, some spots were much hotter than others. Used to the clueless tourist, the young woman pointed at Julie and then the table. Mime works every time.

The rest of us sat and lay on the side benches, spread around the room, feeling for comfortably warm spots. It was obvious the kessel mitt would be used for removing dead skin, and there would be water involved, but the sensation was an unknown. Julie lay still, nervous, while we all watched. The process, repeated for all, but a straight-laced Jay, was the same. A thick-walled, leather bucket was filled with warm water, the sloshing sound echoing loud around the hard walls. The table dweller was then doused in it, a strangely luxurious feeling. The girl delved into a pot of black soap, resembling thick oily grease, and smeared it over the skin. With one hand pressing over the other for weight, the kessel mitt was rubbed over the skin, grey rolls of plasticine-like dead skin, forming, and falling to the floor. Another bucket wash down and, lacking a layer or two of dead skin, the lobster-pink subject would turn over for the other side to be treated. Once scrubbed pink it was time to move from the table, taking care to remember flip-flops as the tiled floor was scorching. Sitting on the side benches hair was shampooed, with more buckets used to rinse it, before the girl left the room.

We couldn't quite work out why she would always leave, the first time we wondered if she would return, but she did after a few minutes. Only afterwards, rinsed in cool water, dried and dressed in the robes did we spot her, sound asleep on the floor in a side room. Exhausted after the manual effort of scrubbing three people in a virtual sauna, she'd retreated to the rooms earlier to cool off.

Tina and Julie would have happily sat in the spa all day, but Chris and Jay were keen to see more of the outside world and more importantly to buy food for the evening's meal. With Tina sleeping off the vigorous scrub, the rest of us, dogs leashed up, headed off. Chris led the way, he'd scouted out a small shop in a village a couple of kilometres away. A dirt track ran north-south along the line of mud-covered hotels. Undulating, cut up and occasionally stopping dead, it was clearly unused by the usual tourist coaches and polished four by fours. The roads in the village were no better, flattened dirt running around blocks of earthy cubes. As in many third world countries, the two extremes of wealth and poverty co-exist peacefully. Along the front of the tiny cafe-shop, a rickety wooden walkway played host to an equally aged table football game. Boys span handles with the passion of world cup final supporters, yelling and pointing.

Keeping the dogs out of the shop, Julie sat on the edge of the walkway. As the game drew to a close, the older boys used the table as cover to peer over at the dogs. Stood with lolling tongues, daft in the warmth, the animals were clearly an unknown and potential source of pain to the boys. Spotting them looking, Julie stroked the dogs, showing they were safe. Slowly the braver ones ventured over and stretched out their hands towards Charlie. Loli being double the height of Charlie, got little attention, despite her grey-flecked black fur and milky eyes telling of her lengthy life. A gaggle of boys now leaned in to stroke Charlie, keeping Julie between them and the unaware Loli. Inside, Chris and Jay confused the shop keeper with fractured French, establishing that the jar of honey he held may, or may not, have come from Morocco. It was good price though, so with flat loaves of bread, some lemon drink, Arabic-scripted wafer-padded chocolate bars and a few bagged-up vegetables, they triumphantly headed outside, to be welcomed back by a leaping Loli. The boy stood closest to the previously docile pooch nearly jumped from his skin at the sight of her rearing up towards him, her teeth glinting in a wolfish grin.

As we started to head back, we saw a campsite sign. The internet being the collective, pervasive thing it is, we knew that fellow travellers and blog writers were holed up there in their rolling homes. As a result of virtual acquaintances, we knew each other more by blog titles than by name: Adam and Sophie were *Europe by Camper*, Catherine and Christopher were *The World is Our Lobster*. They had teamed up in Algeciras in Spain, and travelled in advance of us, taking the country in an anti-clockwise direction, the opposite to us. After working their way down Morocco's Atlantic coast they had headed inland ending up in just a couple of kilometres away from us in the vast desert. We recognised their motorhomes from photographs we had seen on their sites. As we approached them we saw movement in one of the vans, so headed over and knocked on the door.

In this most unlikely of settings, on the edge of a desert, a stones-throw from the Algerian border, it came to pass that we met people whose words over the years had inspired us to get here. We shook hands, hugged and beamed, introducing ourselves. Over a shared pot of mint tea sat in a circle on the campsite's café balcony, we shared stories, while the dogs slept in the shade. All too soon it was time for us to leave, we were booked on a camel ride to watch the sun set, so we arranged to meet later. Their alcohol stocks dry, the promise of beer at the auberge sealed the gathering point and we laughed at the unusual directions: *"head south until you see the two huge camels"*. These guys had travelled the length of Europe, they'd find us. Jay went to pay for the tea, the owner surprising him by asking how much he'd like to pay.

Walking back to the auberge we were accompanied by a group of boys. They were crafty, wily chaps, attempting to show us the way along a path we already knew. We joked with them in French. For some reason, when told the name *Jason*, they all blurted *Michael Jackson?* Hopefully they already knew he had died; if not, they found out that day in the desert. Boys peeled off from the group as we walked further, only those with pared-down bikes stuck it out all the way. As their potential benefactors turned into the auberge entrance, their desperate calls for bonbon, caramelo, one Dirham, all fell on deaf ears. We smiled at them, joked in French they should pay us for guiding them, and waved.

Camel rides on the erg, tacky and touristy as they may be, were a good source of income for the locals. We also figured we couldn't miss out on the opportunity, our only other camel-mounted expedition having been around a mud track in Tenerife. If we were going to do it, we'd do it in style, donning all the Moroccan garb we had, Julie's djellaba had its first outing, as did Jay's Berber coat, both topped off with stunning blue Tuareg scarves, courtesy of Chris and Tina. As Tina wrapped our heads in them, we took photos against the backdrop of the dunes, finding the whole thing hilarious. Standing by the camels we felt a little more self-conscious, adjusting our scarves, until a guide came from the tent, tugged at a rope to bring a camel to its knees and hooked a ruck sack onto a pommel. Julie climbed aboard and leaned backwards as the animal, nicknamed by us

Ermintrude swung backwards and then forwards onto its flat, spongy feet. *Zebedee*, as the lead camel came to be known, invited Jay aboard in the same fashion. Lurching along, we towered high above Omar, our robed guide, who stepped along slowly among the flat ground before the dunes. A train of camels had passed us earlier carrying some of the Japanese tourists we'd shared the buffet with, we counted 25 in total. We had a train of two, and saw no one else, winter is a good time to visit the erg.

Omar's foreign language skills nearly matched our own. Plucking from the *non native words* pool in his head, sentences would drift up to us in a mixture of English, French, German and other unidentified words. Bending to pick up a rounded stone, he passed it to us. It was fossilised camel dung, dried to a rock, it emitted no smell and was pocketed as a souvenir. Looking down we watched as our camel's huge feet spread out when they touched the sand. Omar broke the trance, pointing out that part of Sex and the City II was filmed here, the erg providing a stand in for the Dubai desert, so we were in good company. Omar knew how to manage novice camel riders, leading the train along ridges and switch-backing on steeper dunes. Finding his sunset-watching spot, he hushed the camels down to their knees on a lower, flatter area of sand. As we dismounted Omar took a rope and tied Zebedee's calf to his upper leg, bending it in two. It appeared to us a cruel method, but there was nothing else to tie them to, and an earlier attempt to use a hardy grass clump as an anchor had seen us wandering leaderless.

We climbed to the ridge top, clawing in the soft sand, and sat alongside Omar. The sky changed its coat above us, deep blue in the east, pink-orange to the west. Off to the right a dark cloud rose from the ground, *"It's just a bit of wind, no sandstorm"* Omar assured us. In the twenty minutes we sat waiting for the sun to leave us, Omar spoke easily with us, paying out the tourist message. A local legend says the erg was created by Allah as punishment for the locals because a wealthy couple turned away a tired traveller. In response Allah dropped thousands of tonnes of sand on their home. We asked him if the dunes ever reached the town, as they moved with the wind like a sandy sea, he simply shrugged and said *"sometimes"*.

As the sun dipped, the camels knew it was time to leave. Despite a hobbled front leg they started off, Omar left us to sit close and coo over the changing colours, while he went to retrieve them. Today's sun rise and set, far removed from the day to day long kilometres of concentrated driving, were awe-inspiring, making us long for a magical lottery win to enable a lifetime of such natural wonders.

Omar wasted little time at the camels, the purpose of the rucksack becoming clear as he unwrapped polished inlaid fossils, egg-shaped stones, mini-tagines and ash trays. We'd already encountered this method of selling, as had everyone in our small group. It starts with the phrase *"please, look at my work?"* and ends with you buying a piece of marvellous, heavy stone. Omar showed no sign of disappointment when we changed the ending, explaining we were travelling for months and couldn't take these things with us, no matter how well crafted. As he carefully wrapped back up the camel-men's collective work, we took photos of Zebedee, staring at the hard pad on his underside where he rests his foot when kneeling.

The air cooled quickly as Omar picked out an easy route back through the darkening dunes. A few steeper dunes caught us out, throwing us backwards to stay on board, no stirrups for stability. The scarves we'd felt a little foolish wearing earlier, came into their own, pulled up high as a small wind spat sand in our faces. Even after two hours our legs, unused to the action, ached. We thankfully dismounted, tipped Omar and took off jelly-legged towards Dave. Tina met us before we got in the door, explaining she'd made food for us to eat later, and the bar called.

Our blogging compatriots welcomed us, hands resting against drinks, leaning forwards in discussion. In the group, Catherine and Christopher were undisputed alpha-bloggers, having set themselves a goal to visit all 47 countries in Europe. Three years into the trip, Morocco had been a side-trip they were so far relishing, their beautifully written site, inspired us weekly with their progress. Adam and Sophie were King and Queen of technology and budget trip blogging, coming to the end of a tight-budget, year-long tour. Their site had been mine of fabulously useful, first hand and well-crafted information for us. The conversation swung along, typically honing in on cassette toilet woes, a compulsory topic among any group of motorhomers. Adam's hilarious tale of an exploding loo, caused by pressure differences on a mountain drive, painted a hilarious picture. The beer was cautiously consumed, the one advantage of travelling in an Islamic country is the benefit to one's liver, unless your wallet is fat and open. An hour or two later, slowing like robots on depleted batteries, we agreed to quit, and to meet again the following night. Tina fed us and we fell into Dave's pull-down bed, exhausted and delighted.

The following day we all relaxed. Charlie and Jay's walk in the dunes gave him opportunity to put a demon to rest. The previous day he'd taken a wide detour in order to avoid a promised return to the motorbike-based fossil seller. This time Jay pulled together a few nerves and headed straight for the figure, hand outstretch to shake. The pitch was, as usual, determined and friendly, as was the negative response. The encounter ended in a hug and shaken hands, both men smiling. Moroccans are by necessity tough salespeople, but they're an incessantly easy-going bunch along with it. The seller knowing he wasn't going to sell, popped in a last second request for any spare clothes, but by now we'd already given them away.

The hug with the fossil seller marked a change. Erasing the foolish fear we felt when we entered the country. Unlike Europe, where a typical travelling day can result in speaking not a word to anyone, we were pressed up close here. A continual stream of hopeful sellers of goods and services would walk alongside. Lack of Arabic, Berber, French or any other language is no obstacle, many of them long ago learned linguistic skills, outweighing an ability to read and write. We noted quickly that no-one was drunk here. The fear we felt at night in our home town of those foolish with drink was missing. Unless you were the fool, haggling resulted in, what felt like, a fair price. The hug with the seller was fun, from what would have been, a week ago, a fearful encounter. We felt this the essence of travel.

More hours of the day passed into fruitless kite flying. Chris' wing-like kite wouldn't catch in the minor breeze. Our flailing, running and shouts of encouragement attracted a few local young men who similarly failed, both in flying the kite and buying our remaining bike. Walking past Omar, sat idle at the camels we pointed at the kite: *"no wind"*. Omar responded: *"that is good, wind here is bad"*. We saw his point. As a compromise from nature, we successfully spotted a few dung beetles, black and smooth with powerful long rear legs. They feed on camel faeces, and we watched as they rolled the food in sandy tracks to a suitable burying spot.

After a Dave-based lunch for four, we got back together with the bloggers. Chris and Tina had sweet-talked Hamid into starting a fire for us out on the sands, but as we sat supping in the bar he was nowhere to be seen. A carefully constructed stack of wood in front of the hotel was, we were told, only for hotel guests. We asked for Hamid and a few minutes later he appeared, nodded an affirmation that he would make fire, and instructed someone else to do it. Half a drink later, and he re-appeared and beckoned before walking off into the darkness. Grabbing our glasses we followed out through the camels, snorting indignantly at the interruption to their star gazing. At the camel-men's tent thick blankets were handed out before we were lead over a small dune to a fire, burning out of sight of the hotel. Wood, we realised, is a rare commodity here.

An unknown man, one of several who appeared and disappeared that night, showed us how to wrap the blankets so we also sat on them and covered our bodies. Sitting upwind of the fire, in a semi-circle, we chatted drank our glasses dry beneath a thousand stars. Julie nipped back to the hotel, to pay the bar bill, so we didn't have to hurry back, and grabbed the last box of wine from Dave. As we awkwardly ripped it open and shared it around, two men from the next kasbah north arrived. The owner and a second in command, they carried their own bottle of wine and were already as drunk as we were. With a bit of banter, we discovered they spoke very good English, German, French, Spanish and some Japanese. Questions about Moroccan life which had waited curious in each other's minds popped out. Many had the same answer, accompanied by a wry smile: the *modern Berber* didn't follow all strict Islamic rules to the letter! Chris, a successful businessman himself, wanted to know how this chap had elevated himself to position of hotel owner. *"Not a topic for tonight. Come tomorrow, and we can talk over tea."*

We sat out under the stars until tiredness called us back to our beds. After the long walk back to their campsite last night Adam had decided to drive over. The dejected boys who had tried to guide us back to the Auberge the previous day, finally made a few Dirhams, helping Adam safely navigate the pitch-black non-road to their camp.

FILTHY AND GORGEOUS

Chris never had that conversation over tea, much as he wanted to. We woke the following morning with wood smoke in our nostrils and thick heads. The wide, wooden door to the spa showers was closed, and not wanting to hit the road without the luxury of a never-ending supply of hot water in an opulent brightly tiled shower, we tried reception. An unnecessary apology, after all we were paying next to nothing to stay, and a room key is produced: *"just use the room, bring the key back when you are finished, take your time"*. Once we'd figured out the red-marked golden tap produced cold water, the blue one hot, we each stood in steam and gleamed.

Payment for our stay wasn't the usual process of handing over the cash at reception. Hamid appeared, as if in a puff of smoke, and took the money without counting it, almost as though he felt mildly insulted for his guests needing to pay. Perhaps a long-practised act, we don't know, but the envelope contained a tip as the place was ridiculously cheap, plus he'd come good with the previous night's fire. We shook hands with Hamid and took to our vans, falling comfortably back into the convoy of two that had taken us across Northern Spain and Portugal, walkie talkies crackling with often incomprehensible jokes and instructions, confidence was high. As we drove under the towering arched camels, our path was blocked by a real one, stood astride the dirt track at an angle, glowering at us. Was it trying to tell us not to leave? In a two-van versus dromedary duel, the metal won out as the dusty creature lumbered off indignantly.

The Todra Gorge lay to the west of us, our target for today. That much we'd agreed on, but little else. Walkie talkie garbled conversation lined us up: we needed cash, no-one in Morocco we dealt with accepted anything but paper and coins. The grey water situation was also a problem; the tanks slung under the vans used to catch washing water were brimming full. Ordinarily, emptying this washing-up liquid and soap mix onto the ground is just not on, but in an African desert, there wasn't much choice. We stopped and slightly opened the taps which let the water start to dribble out, and set off again, trailing the stuff over a long distance to dilute it among the dust and dirt.

Entering Rissani, the jumping off point for the Erg Chebbi, everyone stared around for a cash point within the jumbled, haphazard life of the place. Instead of the keyboard and screen, a couple of European faces peered out of the crowd, poking the air in our direction with their thumbs. Having failed to pick up a single Moroccan, we found ourselves waiting a little further along the road as the smiling faces heaved ruck-sacks through the crowd and climbed into the van. Françoise and Estelle spoke less English than we spoke French, so we used the latter to discover they were on their way to Marrakech for a flight home in three days. They wanted to stop off at the gorge, despite having a huge distance to cover.

Setting off again, Chris and Tina's van was no longer behind us. The walkie talkie told us they'd found a cash point and would catch us up. With a four hour drive ahead of us, and Christina being a little bit newer and faster than Dave, we felt sure we'd spot them approaching in our mirror at some point. Our hitch-hikers, all dreadlocks and faded climbing clothes, struggled to hear us in the rumbling depths of the van. Julie made good with mime and dipped into nurse mode, finding eye drops for Françoise, who's eyes were bright red from blown sand. In return the young couple marked places for us to visit near their home town on our French map. With a bit to eat, they drifted off, Françoise almost upright, leaning against his ruck sack, and Estelle stretched on the bench seat. Charlie had taken to them both, and lay at the bottom of the bench in a ball, snoring beside Estelle's feet.

Our sleeping hitch-hikers missed out on more stunning scenery. Like a dishevelled beard, tiny black palms lined either side of the yellow road on our now-tearing map. *Moulay-Brahim, Achouria, Ba Touroug,* the town names sounded French, enhanced by a desert tongue. Through a miles-wide flat valley, we sailed along past the dead, red and cracked rocks resting in dust. A Moroccan man, stood waiting for who-knows-what, resembled a redundant scarecrow in the crop-less scorched earth. Either side the mountains shrugged upwards. The road, straight as a plumb-line, grumbled as we rolled along.

We quickly learned that small red and white painted concrete sand-castles lining the road signalled a rough patch. As we slowed down to avoid the inconvenience of a removed wheel, the bone-dry tumble of white rounded rocks explained all. When the rain fell or snow melted on the mountains the water used these marked places to escape over the road, pulling tarmac-mashing boulders along with it. Photographs we looked at on the internet that evening, showed impatient buses and lorries that had been taught a lesson by the flood. Washed off the road, they hung in thin air or lay prone on one side in the again-dry river bed. Françoise and Estelle awoke and rummaged for dog-eared books, comfortable in silence as Dave banged into yet another pot-hole and Jay quietly swore.

With the hours behind us, we approached Tinerhir, the turning point for the Todra Gorge. A bit of dialogue established that Françoise and Estelle were happy to be dropped off at the campsite we were staying at. Being hard-floored dust and muck affairs, we saw very few people actually camp in Moroccan campsites. They were invariably filled with retirees in a comfortably apportioned glinting white motorhome, or some other slightly lesser van-based life-form. Our French riders hoped to rent a bungalow on the site, or a room nearby. Our plan to drive to the site together was immediately changed as the sign for the Todra Gorge, pointed the opposite way to the Shat-nav's insistent green line. With a quick handshake, Françoise and Estelle jumped from the van with their bags, and loped along back towards the sign.

A few hundred metres later, parked alongside the dusty road in the middle of a town, we bared our teeth as Shat-nav chirped in her usual dulcet tone *"make a u-turn"*. Tinerhir high street was fairly quiet and we managed to turn around, without bumping a laden donkey or heaving bus. Looking for the hitch-hikers as we drove the right road towards the campsite and Gorge, there was no sign of them. Maybe they got picked up straight away, or had nipped into a shop, whatever happened, we never saw them again.

The road towards the Gorge was white on our map, one up from dirt. On this particular stretch of highway it meant the black top has been eaten by the hungry earth, leaving a rough-edged strip of it down the centre wide enough for a car. Passage was fine, and we entertained ourselves with intermittent two-wheeled off-roading forays as another car approached. Either side of the unloved route, dwellings of mud attempted to stay upright, further evidence of the crayon-wielding child-architect's work we'd witnessed on our journey south. Spiked green palm leaves mingled with blossom in areas where water was persuaded to flow. Only minarets were painted, cream towers reaching above the cubed houses beneath. The flat red earth thrust upwards around it all, as though a mythical mole shoved away beneath. We had strayed back into the foothills of the High Atlas.

Our campsite had competition. With the exception of Erg Chebbi and Fes, each town we'd visited had a single *camping*. Passing a couple of them confirmed we were in a well-visited spot, positioned as it was roughly half way between Marrakech and the dunes. Flags, drooping in the breeze-less sun, marked the entrance. Passing the painted metal gates the place felt welcoming and warm. After parking Dave under palms and in the shade of a tall cliff, Julie inspected pink-coloured buildings, reporting back, with a beam: a working washing machine, and usable showers.

Chris and Tina pulled in alongside us half an hour later, their fridge packed full after a shopping trip. That evening Tina saved us from yet another cous-cous or meat tagine, with a skillet-roasted moist chicken and vegetables. It was accompanied by a stowaway bottle of port, which we'd discovered, along with a fellow-stowaway bottle of sherry, while rummaging through dirty clothes in preparation for a laundry run. Once a suitable amount of the crimson liquid had been consumed, Jay revealed a small truth about two wired off hollows in the cliff bottom nearby, earlier sniffed-out by Charlie. They were full of rabbits - too full, and not all of them were still alive. We'd seen enough casually-left dead animals during our time in Morocco, so decided to steer clear.

The old washing machine had taken over two hours to wash Tina's load of clothes, perhaps explaining why so much washing was still done by hand. Knowing this Julie leapt out of bed the following morning as the sun was still brightening the sky, and the air was still chilled. Her plan was to get the washing on and get back into bed. Jay didn't know this plan, and thought Julie would be happy to return to Dave and find him up and eating breakfast, the bed made and pushed back into its place above the cab. This land wasn't a place for sleeping, but for excitement and discovery, at least it was for Jay at 7am. Disappointed, Julie kept an eye on the languishing clothes, making sure the machine drank the fabric softener, as each spin sloshed out a tiny bit of water from the bodged door.

The desert air was taking its toll on our bodies, rolling abode and pooch. As it leached every last drop of moisture from skin, it also charged man-made fibres and fur, both of which there was a lot of in Dave. Not comprehending the concept of static electricity, Charlie yelped as tiny sparks shot like a punishment into his inquisitive wet nose, his fur standing to attention as he lay on his fleece blanket. As the washing machine finally finished its marathon session, the campsite took on the look of a Tibetan hillside, trees adorned with lines of hanging prayer-clothes. Leaving the sun to work its magic we all piled into Dave and set off up the gorge beneath another perfect-blue sky.

The last 600m of the 40km long gorge, carved through the High Atlas by the river Todra, are said to be the most spectacular. However, we had no idea where this section of the gorge started. As we drove alongside the tame Todra, red rock rising around us, we felt as if we were already in a gorge. Reaching a town, Julie spotted a white mini bus with a hand-written *Touristique* sign in the window. This must be it, we pulled in next to it and jumped out, watched closely by a few leaning locals. Waiting for the inevitable *guardien* to arrive in high-visibility officiousness, no-one appeared. Looking around us we had parked in the mosque car park, oops, but as no-one appeared interested in anything but the two tethered dogs we led along with us, we set off on foot.

The road took us about a kilometre before we reached the gorge proper. Loli and Charlie, ever the ice-breakers, had us stopping, chatting with fascinated locals. One lad asked if Charlie was a dog, we eyed him up wondering if he was joking but saw no sign of it. Above us on a cliff of red rock, white painted Arabic writing flowed, in praise to Allah we assumed, rather than advertising Coca Cola. The rising sides of the gorge pushed towards one-another, towering high above a narrow gap, maybe just 10 meters apart. An incongruous floor of concrete smoothed-off the valley bottom, trickling alongside it today's Todra seemed nothing, surely incapable of ever cutting the high rock channel?

Where the rock wall met the concrete, hanging lines and wheeled wooden carts stood empty of sellers, scarves, fossils and pots. A donkey took a few stumbling steps in the dry river bed, an obvious photo opportunity with no-one ready to leap in and request a few Dirhams. It seemed it pays to be both early, and off season. Rope-carrying tourists walked past us unspeaking, off to one of the 150-odd bolted routes up the cliff side. A Moroccan car pulled slowly to one side and a family climbed out, the boys in jeans immediately fooling around on the rocks. Jay was sporting his Berber jacket, and Chris decided this was a suitable time to don his deep blue Tuareg head scarf, which suited him much better than us. As Tina tied it, one of the boys fell from the rocks in a clamour, his face a picture of held-back tears as he retreated around the corner to repair his pride.

Wandering along the bottom of the towering gorge, our necks aching as we looked up at the walls of rocks above, we were surprised to see a hotel and restaurant sitting in its depths. It obviously wasn't put there for passing trade and looked almost comical, as if someone had put it there for a joke. As the walls widen out again, passing more empty shacks awaiting skilled and tenacious owners, we crossed the dry river bed. We followed a worn mud trail, among small uneven patches of land, tufted with tired, struggling crops, which took us below the climbing routes. The group who had passed us sat below, beginners, being literally shown the ropes on the lowest section of cliff. High above them the more experienced looked small against the red cliff face.

As the mud path petered out, we aimlessly wandered along the rough, dry river bed. A jaw bone of some long-dead creature attracted our attention. Unsure of what it had been, the teeth, which refused to fall out, identified it afterwards as a camel. Fleeting shapes dodged like shadows among large rocks closer to the far bank. Creeping towards them, the small scruffy light brown ground squirrels held still long enough for Jay to get a photo. The sun warmed us as we sat in the river bed, our backs against a huge rock, breathing air tinged with a floating wood smoke. A breeze picked up dust and spun it around us, time to go. We climbed out of our river bed onto the road that had wound out from the narrow gorge, and followed it back.

The gorge had woken. Two motorhomes drove past us, on the concrete road, turned around, and headed back out, not bothering to step outside, the view from their windows was enough. Where we had feared a dangerous dirt track, the concrete road ushered full-sized tourist coaches into the deepest section of the gorge, delivering its punters straight to the best bit. With the arrival of the coaches, the sellers had woken too: *"camel bone necklace? Look good on you?"*. Deftly fending the flogger off, we instead expended our Dirhams on Chris' favourite tipple, the *'cheeky mint tea'* as he called it. Cleverly up-sold to food, we ordered plates of chips which, as often seemed the case here, came cold. We ate them anyway, they were delicious.

Making our way back to Dave we passed a shop. The place was tiny, its doorway filled by the obligatory counter. Unable to see what was for sale, Tina asked if she was allowed inside. The locals would know exactly what they wanted, and with a choice of one or none, never needed to venture in. Nevertheless, the shop keeper happily lifted the barrier and Tina craned her neck at the unfamiliar brands on wall-high shelves. Our alcohol supplies were dwindling, only a cheap bottle of sherry remained. We fretted at the possibility of running out of precious liquid like the bloggers in the desert. But in a shop frequented by locals and passed by the tourist buses there was no chance of any form of alcohol. Tina bought round loaves of bread, a toast fetish had developed in Christina.

In the film *Coming to America*, Eddie Murphy, the naive prince, returns to his limousines to find the locals wandering around in his finery, someone runs past with his solid gold hair dryer. Drawing closer to the mosque, Julie voiced her concerns we might find the same scene played out, but with less gold. Chris, pointed out that when shops are closed, they simply drape a blanket across the doorway, no doors or locks: *"These people aren't thieves"* he reassured, *"they may fleece you when you buy something, but that's your own fault for having no business sense"*. Religion holds strong here, along with it an enduring and tangible sense of community. He doubted very much any of them would dare to bring shame on their families by stealing. He was right, Dave stood untouched.

That afternoon, walking Charlie Jay spotted a robed man riding a small motorbike along the broad white arid river bed. His feet stabbed at the ground, just keeping him upright, as his wheels bounced from rounded cobble to cobble. Ahead of him were many more people, this time walking. Women wrapped in white pattered fabric, resembling bed sheet togas, carried tagines, men in jeans, hands in pockets and children throwing stones all heading in the same direction. Abandoning Charlie back at Dave, Jay joined the small throng. As the river throttled down into a small gorge, it's sides just a few meters high, people had taken to side paths and stood chatting in groups either side of the river. With no obvious reason for being there, it looked as if the entire town had turned out, standing chatting. But for a friendly shout from a plastic-leather jacketed youth, no-one paid any attention to the English interloper, Jay turned back, flummoxed.

That evening, Chris encouraged us to abandon the campsite restaurant, and search out somewhere to eat in a near-by string of closed-looking buildings. We ambled along the road in the dark, moonlight shining through palms The first eaterie we came to was enclosed in another campsite, the second was just closed, it's plain metal door bolted shut, but a friendly face waved us into a door further along. The large room, with grey concrete walls had a partition down the centre to separate eating and cooking areas. A picture of the King half-smiled at us, seemingly adopting a kind of Mona Lisa pose. Four white plastic garden tables surrounded by empty chairs filled the eating half. The cool night air pushed us to the table farthest from the door in the hope of some warmth, but it never arrived, we sat wrapped up in our coats all evening, above us Jimi Hendrix stared down from a faded poster.

Our waiter, who was also our chef, explained all was quiet as there was a festival in town. Jay's earlier foray had only unveiled the warm up to the main event. Glasses of mint tea and warm sugared milk arrived on a circular plain tray, eagerly gripped and sipped to extract warmth from them. Bowls of fresh salad were followed by skewers of crispy grilled chicken and browned thin cut chips. The latter arrived salted and piping hot, giving cause for a small *hooray* of celebration. Desert was plain and simple: a bowl of oranges, delicious and probably sourced from within walking distance. The bill came to around £6.50 per person. We could get used to this.

The locked gates at the campsite caused a small delay in our return. Unsure whether the owner was miffed at our avoidance of his restaurant, or whether he simply forgot to tell us the gates get locked when he'd opened it to let us out, Chris quickly sussed a way to open one of them. With our silent halogen heater shining all night, we slept warm with full stomachs, wondering what the next day might bring.

Listening to Chris Evans in the morning, we felt a pang of homesickness until the traffic report. Ice was causing havoc on the A1. Cars we queuing for hours. We looked outside at the crisp light streaming through the palms and bouncing from the red cliff above and all homesickness evaporated. Sniffing at the freshness of our now-dry washing, we packed it away and left the site in convoy. Christina followed Dave, as Dave followed Shat-nav. With a sense of direction as developed as a dizzy spaniel, she was of debatable benefit. She rarely agreed with the spelling of town names on our map; to her the *A*s, *E*s and *I*s were seemingly interchangeable, she would take or leave apostrophes, and when she was feeling particularly annoying she'd use a completely different town name altogether. All too soon Shat-nav tired of the long drives, brightening them up by calmly insisting we turn left, straight into the desert or creating inexplicable gaps in main roads so she could help by navigating us around them.

Our destination today was the next major tourist spot towards Marrakech, the Dades Gorge. Photographs of the road scrambling in a series of concertina switch-backs adorn guide books and posters. The drivers were nervous, but maybe not as nervous as the passengers though. Driving back along the torn strip of tarmac, windows closed against the cool air, butterflies fearing the future were replaced, once again, with acute concentration in the present. The drive today was relatively short. Bouncing our way back to the main road, we reached Tinerhir, now busy with a used car and tractor market. A couple of men caught our attention as they walked along the road holding hands. Homosexuality remains illegal in Morocco, this was simply a sign of friendship, but not something we'd ever seen in public. Leaving the town, the road smoothed and we travelled quickly, by Moroccan standards.

Yet more jaw-dropping scenery played out through our increasingly-murky windows, we started to dull to it. The thrill of the colours and light washing over us for the first time was ever-present, but had calmed from a blood-rush to a quiet admiration, like a new love. Far from anything, walled towers stood either side of the road, painted pink with white decoration in blocky lego-like shapes they marked territories and borders we knew nothing of. Ahead of us a group of men stood around a car, bonnet up, one of them attempting to flag passing vehicles down. With miles of desert around, our first instinct was to stop and help, but a warning bell rang. A common scam is pretending to have broken down in order to get a lift into the next town. Once there, with arms waving in feigned gratitude, the rescuer would be taken to a relatives shop where a great discount would be offered. Harmless, but annoying. Fortunately before we arrived at the scene a lorry pulled in to help out; it seemed their plight was real.

Boulmalne Dades plays the same part as Tinerhir along this section of the N10 tourist trail, a thriving, if functional town in its own right, but for us it was simply a signal to turn north into the High Atlas. Next to a roundabout a square building sat with its door open, spilling out through it was a tide of white UPVC windows, *Aluminium Dades* read the neat sign. Openings are made to fit the glass here, not the other way around. The road snaked up into the gorge. Past decaying kasbahs and stunning rock formations, one of which rushed at us, crowds of giants angrily charging along the side of the river.

Two men worked by the roadside, building a house, balancing high in the air on teetering planks of wood held in place by pretty much nothing. Small piles of stones or thrusting dried palm leaves cropped up along the edge of the tarmac, the only indication of a missing section large enough to snap a wheel or turn us tumbling off into the valley below. We drove along the centre of the road like the local taxis and vans, our love-to-hate European Health and Safety laws are clearly seen as either a luxury, or a nonsense. As the valley deepened, the road clawed along its right side, the drop off thankfully shielded by a low wall. A red warning triangle lifted our gaze, the wall slashed back and forth at ever-increasing heights through the rock towering above, itself tilted into steep layers. Our hearts thumped.

Minutes later our vans parked alongside one another, we'd driven the section of hairpins easily and smoothly. The photographs of the Dades Gorge don't lie, they just don't tell the full truth. They tease into believing the road is an endless challenge, flinging back and forth across kilometres of precipitous cliff. A mere five or six hairpins joined by short sections of smooth wide road and it's all over; we felt part relief and part disappointment. A café poised over the top of the road held the prime photography spot, this fact coupled with hunger drew us in for a huge family-sized tagine of cous-cous, squishy vegetables and bony chicken. The café also had an unusual picture of the King. Rather than his usual front-of-flag pose he was be-suited and shaking hands with someone, not the café owner we discovered, but his friend.

As we walked back to the vans the café owner offered to let us sleep in his car park; we thanked him but declined. The wind blew up here, and we'd spotted restaurants in the valley, with a *camping* sign, meaning they had a car park we could use alongside the river. Despite our earlier cavalier attitude towards the short concertina section of the road, we took it easy on the descent, more fearful of burning brakes than anything else. A short distance along the flat section of road found a likely-looking restaurant and hotel. Painted pink concrete threes stories high stood still while the flags of likely tourist countries fluttered outside; even the Union Flag made an appearance. The owner stood outside, as though he had nothing better to occupy him, and earnestly welcomed us in, showing us the toilets and proudly pointed to the log fire in the wide-open restaurant; *"it will be lit tonight"*.

On agreement that we bought a meal, we could stay in his car park opposite for free. The vans were manoeuvred into place, end-on into the wind, but dog walking potential was found to be lacking. The rivers here are reputed to carry bilharzia parasite which enters through the skin. Unsure what it was exactly, or what ill-wanted results contracting it might have, Charlie's walk was confined to the road. A couple of stray dogs stalked the car park, one looking like it may have just discharged a pack of pups. Another had an sore on its forehead, causing us to wince in sympathy. The valley filled with shadow early, the sun disappearing behind the red cliff walls. We shivered, unwilling to turn on up our gas-fired heating, we had no idea how long the contents of the LPG tank we had might last. LPG is unheard of in Morocco.

Luckily the fire was, as promised, roaring with flame when we sat down for dinner. Among the ten or so tables, only three were occupied, the other two by Moroccan families. Nods acknowledged each other, but we didn't speak, we quietly watched them from time to time, in case of any extraordinary behaviour. Given the sobriety, there was none. We, on the other hand, ordered a bottle of red wine, for a price roughly five times what we'd pay in the UK. Moroccan wines are an acquired taste, we much preferred the budget boxes of Spanish wine, but they were now gone, bartered and sunk. The food was good, our conversation becoming less muted with the wine, we swapped places around the table half way through to share the heat of the fire. A huge bowl of fruit arrived for desert, but after two big meals in one day we were full. As we'd ordered from a set menu we'd end up paying for the fruit anyway, so we each ate a piece and pocketed a couple more. Pockets bulging, we pottered back down the stairs and into respective vans, falling asleep almost immediately to the sound of the river a few meters away.

In the base of the gorge, walls towering above, the night was cold. We woke at one point to find Charlie curled into the tightest of balls, his static-inducing fleece blanket having been confiscated earlier. One of our layers, a grey sleeping bag, was flung from the bed over him and we dozed back off, only to wake a few hours later in the chilly half-light, the sun would rise late over the other cliff, so the gas heating went on. When we finally ventured out, it was still early and cold, the wild dogs were fed scraps by both Tina and Jay, out of sympathy. Once they had food they turned vicious, and we were glad to leave.

We headed back down the road take a closer look at the humanoid rock formations we'd spotted on the way into the gorge. Chris found a lay-by and pulled in, to Julie's consternation, it was an hour's walk from the rocks. Chris and Tina had recently tandem-ridden from Lands End to John

O'Groats to raise money for a cancer charity; an hour's walking was nothing. To Julie it was a K2 conquest and her face showed it. We drove closer and found an area of land rough enough to bounce our heads on the ceiling as we pulled in.

The orange figures of bobbled rock hunched together on the opposite side of the river. Still low, the sun cast healthy shadows and crept up over the heads of the imagined crowd. As we hunted about for a route to take us down from the rough rounded rocks to the river, a local man walked straight off the edge of an apparent cliff, appearing unharmed at a small hut below. Shaking our heads in disbelief and to confirm our joint intention not to follow, we took a longer path. Passing a house which doubled up as a farm, chickens scratched around outside attracting the attention of our leashed pooches, we picked up some company. Two young boys, maybe eight years old, fulfilled the role of the urchin, pestering us to show us *la route*. Doing our best to ignore them, we walked, wondering whether this land alongside the river was somehow private, a concept a little alien in rural, desert Morocco.

With a camera full of photos, we headed back, urchins still in tow. As it became clear to them that their prey was escaping, the boys demands gushed out, becoming ever more urgent. Pens, sweets, toys, shoes, paper, Dirhams, and even Charlie were demanded in payment for, well, nothing. By this point Jay, the best French speaker, was alone with them, the others having hot-footed it back to the vans. Dredging up school day French he admonished the boys: *go to school, learn something, get a job*. Their eyes were downcast for a second, before the begging recommenced. Elevating his voice to a near shout seemed to do the trick: *non, enough!* Giving the children here something for nothing is turning them in an entire generation of beggars. Not good for Morocco, or for their future.

A SHORT SOJOURN SOUTH

Ouarzazate describes itself as the *'door of the desert'*, a major town at the confluence of the Draa and Dades valleys. Not yet ready to leave the refreshing expanses of nothing and head back over the High Atlas, we'd agreed on another swing south.

Crossing 100 kilometres of desert plateau, our grey water trickled out a path in greasy lines as the spectacular snow-headed peaks to our right stared down. Gritted teeth carried us over sections of waterway-road, the van banging and grinding in consternation when we incorrectly judged the amount of slowing needed. More middle-of-nowhere pink-painted towers told us we'd crossed another unknown boundary.

On the outskirts of Ouarzazate, the road eased downwards into clusters of blocky brown buildings, facing all directions like pixelated meercats. A familiar police road block brought our eyes back to the road, battered white signs informing us we must stop. We duly halted and, as ever, were waved through. The bleedle-beep on our walkie-talkie announced a laughing Tina who relayed the news we'd almost washed an unsmiling policemen's shoes with a glug of sulphurous grey water. Deciding it probably wasn't a good idea to stop there to turn it off, we ploughed on.

The campsite in town was a familiar affair, high walled, packed earth and packed with French and German motorhomes. Julie returned from checking-in duty a little bemused. The man on reception had refused her passport details, requesting only those of a male. Women, we knew, had few rights in Morocco. Western ideas of equality are completely alien here, but it was no issue for us interlopers, Julie just handed over the other passport.

We decided to walk into town, but before we left there was a plea for help from Chris and Tina. After dropping and breaking their hob-top kettle, their electric one had now given up the ghost. Chris' manly attempt to fix it, had near-frazzled him with a shock. The only thing consumed in greater quantities than toast in Christina, was tea. A constantly boiling kettle was

112

now missing from the picture, so we handed over our hob-top one, our tiny electric kettle would be ample for our occasional coffees.

Leaving Chris and Tina to a cuppa, or two, we headed off. Ouarzazate is the largest town in Saharan Morocco and was once a crossing point for African traders seeking to reach the northern cities in Morocco and Europe. During the French occupation it expanded as a garrison town and administrative centre and we soon found that our campsite was on the outskirts. Stood at a large roundabout, one road leading back to the campsite, another to the Dades Gorge, we looked for a reassuring *'Centre Ville'* sign on one of the other two options, but there wasn't one. A policeman leaning against a mini-bus of his colleagues pointed the way, smiling. After a twenty minute walk all we found were tiny bland little shops, no sign of a market, cafés or larger shops. Another twenty minutes, including a detour into an Arabic-signed pastry shop, and we finally found the town.

Passing a couple of banks, the road opened out wide, making room for the inflated egos of shining hotels. Amongst the well known names stood a kasbah-styled hotel, adorned with white bed sheet banners painted in Arabic and French. We understood *A Vendre, For Sale*, but it explained little. The windows and doors stood closed, lifeless but for a rough camp of men under a tarpaulin. Summoning non-existent courage we encouraged Charlie across the street and asked a few questions. It transpired the builders had gone bust. These were the craftsmen who had built it and now sat in guard, for over a year, to ensure they received their payment.

At this point we were lost, turned around in the dusty wide streets. Julie had wisely noted the campsite's location, on Avenue Muhammed V. Asking hotel porter where it was prompted a look of confusion, *you're already on it, this is the road.* Walking along it we passed the Kasbah of Taourirt, a rambling affair which faced the road on one side and backed into the desert on the other. The polished entrance door was locked. Finally arriving at the familiar roundabout we realised that the town was actually down the other road, not the one the policeman had pointed us to - we wondered where he thought we wanted to go.

Back at the campsite we found Chris, holding our slightly melted kettle and smiling nervously, it had boiled dry as they snoozed. Three kettles in three days we smiled, his new nickname - the kettle killer.

The following morning we made a discovery: Moroccan pastries offer more the promise of a filling than any actual filling. The apple turnover was fruitless and the pain-au-chocolat, was just a pain. Determined to get something right, the four of us set off on a mission to buy kettles. In the land of the mint tea, almost every souvenir shop sold tea pots, but we wanted fat shiny kettles. We eventually found them stacked high, literally. The white-robed lady shop owner struggled to reach them from their vantage point on the highest of shelves. Before handing one over she blew in the spout, a harmonica buzz erupted from the kettle top, we tried to hide our enthusiasm for such a fabulous feature. Chris was investing in two kettles that day, one for himself and one for us, the matching kettles would be a great reminder of our trip. Checking we liked the design and receiving a resounding thumbs-up, he took up the haggling reigns. Fifteen minutes later, with Tina exiting the shop part way through in amazement at the tiny amounts being argued over, the deed was done. Outside the kasbah, feeling a little giddy, Chris and Jay danced a daft jig to the tune of two one-note harmonica kettles, providing amusement for a near-by security guard.

A *cheeky mint tea* was called for. The flaking paint of an orange 100cc motorbike parked outside a café gave Jay cause to pause. Within seconds the owner sprang and we settled around a shining table, observing the assortment of weird and wonderful vehicles jostling along the road behind. Asking the owner for a look at his bike, he practically threw Jay onto it and, while running and pushing, demonstrated the starting action. Lurching into life the bike stretched out an involuntary idiot grin on Jay's face as he pootled back and forth in front of the tables. The feeling of riding a bike without a helmet was an alien one to him, and he quite simply loved it. The owner had maybe seen some glint in his eye and had dutifully exploited it, earning a good tip and an earnest handshake as we left.

As Jay filled Dave with fresh water ready for the day's trip desertwards, Julie and Tina made another trip to the campsite's tiny office. Returning a few minutes later, a recurring problem: no change. Campsites, cafés, shops, museums, they never have enough coins. We had been thinking it was one big scam but the campsite turned the tables by accepting less than the amount due, it seemed there were just too few coins to go around.

Our convoy of two sailed south, the roadside buildings quickly replaced by building materials, rocks, dust and earth. Fluttering in impatience, trapped against scabby trees and the edges of boulders, a veritable sea of plastic bags demanded we look at them. We stared back, not speaking. The road had a reputation for impressive scenery; this scarred section of it had us thoughtful.

The Tizi-n-Tinififft pass rises five hundred meters above Ouarzazate, and none of us knew how to pronounce it. Before the climb, our route cut a flat, straight line across another plateau, the Romans couldn't have made it any straighter. A man attempted to flag us down, one arm held aloft, stranded. We were naturally inclined to help, until we saw his motorbike propped up against a rock, almost out of sight. The road climbed, sliced into the side of a dead hill, no traffic shared the route giving the drivers time to cast a wide eye to the north. After half an hour switching between second and third gear, and back again, a lay-by broke out from the confines of the road. Stood with arms and hands loose at our sides, an astonishing beauty lay below, a simplicity of dead earth, rippling mountain and vibrant clear sky. Finally taking nothing more from the view, a grey-blue beetle, each strutting leg made of three angled sections, marched with intent across the rocks. It seemed this land wasn't entirely dead.

A change of gear signalled the summit. We stopped almost immediately and took the opportunity to gaze along the Draa Valley towards our evening target of Agdz. Djebel Kissane, the *resting place*, rose up as a mountain above the other hills, its name derived from the caravans which would travel of old between Marrakech and Timbuktu. Around it enigmatic swirling ridges played about on the mountains and hills, like combed wet hair. The earth's palette of brown, orange, red and green, was like a fashionable pyjama fabric. We felt light-headed, giddy with joy as we sat on a broken topped wall posing for photos with Charlie looking aghast, fearful of falling as Jay held him to his chest.

Ignoring another non-broken-down car, we flowed off the hills and into Agdz. What would be a one-donkey town in much of the world, was saved by a reliance on the rough-haired beasts for hauling goods. The tiny place thronged with them. Dust whisked around as we rocked along a holed track; our Shat-nav placed us in a white wilderness and abruptly gave up for the day. Tina had been paying attention and spotted a sign for the campsite, and we followed them in. Coming to a gap in the long white-washed wall, we found Gale. She and her Moroccan husband, own and operate *Camping Kasbah de al Palmerie*. Gale, who was from France, graciously complimented us on our awful French and spoke to us in fluent English while booking us in. Exiting the campsite office, we'd happily been up-sold a tour of the adjacent Kasbah, which was owned by Gale's husband's family, and a family-sized tagine of grub, to be delivered to our van later.

Chris, we should explain, is among the most outgoing people on the planet. Speaking fluent German, within minutes he'd struck up conversation with the owner of what might best be described as an *adventure wagon*. We'd seen a few of these beasts on our trip, worrying needlessly that one was needed simply to scoot between Moroccan towns. Rough and rugged from the outside, with enormous tyres, tiny high-up windows and ranks of pale green metal fuel cans, Chris got us all a look at one on the inside, where it was a picture of luxury. Warm wood and cool fabrics made the space light, airy and welcoming belying the rugged exterior. For a cool €100,000, one could be ours, along with a *blind-the-sun* array of *cook-your-intruder* emergency lights mounted outside. Chris wanted one, badly. He wanted to drive the silk route, the generic name for a number of exotic pathways extending about 4000 miles from Europe to China. Tina was perhaps a little less interested, but Chris had a far-away look in his eyes.

Parked up near the beast was Claude and his family, our new friend who'd arranged our guide in Fez. Smiling and holding out his hand to shake, he insisted on sharing his last couple of small cans of cold beer with us. Sitting in his van, his boys creating havoc with toy dinosaurs, Claude and his wife told us they were off on another trip. Selling their food shop in France, their home, their cars, everything, they were moving lock, stock, to St Martin in the Caribbean. *"Why?"* we asked. *"For the adventure, of course?"* came the unexpected response. Sipping the valuable beer, our mouths slightly ajar in admiration, we mangled the French language a little more before saying our *au revoirs*. They left the next day, and sadly we didn't see them again.

It took two people to carry the tagine to Dave that evening, Gale and another woman. Lifting the heavyweight cracked-pot lid with a trembling arm, the cous-cous steam filled the air. Charlie could hardly contain himself, his twitching nose sucking in delicious aroma like a vacuum cleaner. Chicken fell from the bone and we dared one another to take more of the anonymous raging hot red paste supplied in a little pot. By now we were out of all forms of alcohol apart from the cheap bottle of sherry, which we quaffed and shrugged.

The following morning our small tour group assembled. Roger and Sandy, the other British couple on the campsite, joined us, and fulfilled the roles of eccentric wanderers beautifully. Tall, spaced palms towered over the area behind the motorhomes, we walked silently into this oasis of shade following Gale, expecting to turn left into a side door of the mud and whitewash Kasbah Caid Ali. Gale had different ideas, coming to a halt, turning around and, with her hands held clasped in front of her, caught our attention with a *"Welcome to the palmerie!"*. Unexpected facts poured out as we eye-balled the plain-looking ground around us with respect. Water was encouraged to leave the river and seep into the ground here through a series of small mud channels called *seguias*. Crossing neighbours' land, small wooden boards were used to control the flow of water, a sharing system which worked well, with a few inevitable disputes over time. No patch of land was wasted. They seemed to grow practically every fruit bearing tree and plant, including strawberries, grapes, apples, peaches, figs, oranges and, obviously, dates. Unkempt areas of land it turned out were being used to grow fodder for animals. Each new palm tree would, in order to build up a sufficient network of roots, not break the surface of the earth for four years. Palmerie's clearly took some planning.

The Draa Valley is famous for its kasbahs. Fashioned from mud, they're perpetually disintegrating, as we'd seen in Meski. Using the profit from the campsite and tours, renting out rooms in the complex itself, and by using free labour from a University interested in mud buildings, Gale and her husband had cleverly maintained the place. It also served as their home alongside some of their extended family. Moving inside the kasbah, and into its cool, shaded rooms, Gale explained that this kasbah, like many others in Southern Morocco was home for a family unit, like a country house for the middle classes. The ground floor was used for agricultural purposes, although the rooms now stood empty. The upper floors served as living quarters in winter (upper portion) and summer (lower portion). She told us how some kasbah can be veritable palace-fortresses or the seat of local power, taking on the dimensions of a small village.

Gale firstly showed us the rooms which would be seen by visitors of old. Shaded and decorated with coloured patterns painted straight onto the walls and ceilings, now faded with age. Not only to make the visitors feel comfortable and welcome, the use of expensive colours and tiles also demonstrated wealth. Furniture was kept to a minimum and the floor simply covered in rugs. On the roof were two reception areas pointing in different directions so guests could be met in shade at any time of the day. In times gone by, visitors would normally only be in the house for three days. The first to recover from their journey. The second to tell you why they have come to see you, on the premise that no-one travelled unless they had a problem they needed to solve. The third was for resolving the issue and preparing to leave; any longer was seen as imposing. You would also be expected to reciprocate with a visit to their home within a year, or if you couldn't make it then someone would go on your behalf.

Old life in the kasbah sounded good. A couple would be given a small room or apartment when they were married, and would move into bigger ones with each child they had, or each additional wife the man took. As the children left home they would uncomplainingly move back into smaller parts of the building. Wives would rotate duties on a weekly basis, cooking, cleaning, childcare and washing. It all sounded very well organised, if a little strange, to us.

In one room the floor was covered with drying dates. As Gale was French, and therefore had a strong link to our European western attitudes, we felt more open with her, asking questions with less shyness. *"How much should we pay for a packet of dates about this big?"* we asked, indicating the side of a box we'd seen in the nearby town. She smiled and explained that the Draa valley is famous as the date basket of Morocco. This area of arid desert grows more than eighteen varieties, so the cost would depend on which ones you bought, some were obviously much better quality than others. We tried two of the different varieties that had dried, we couldn't tell the difference.

Finally Gale talked us through the restoration of the Kasbah, several people were helping and also using it to teach about traditional building methods. She pointed to rows of new mud bricks drying in the sun, bits of straw sticking out at odd angles. The Kasbah had come to be so badly in need of restoration, because her husband's grandfather was a lord who owned 600 square kilometres of land; which roughly equated to everything you could see from the building's roof.

Unfortunately when he died it was during a time of change in the country. The King was willing to grant ownership of the land to the next lord, but his three sons couldn't decide who it should be. They took so long the King died, the agreement was forgotten, and they lost all of the land; only managing to keep the Kasbah. So now instead of around 200 family members living in it, there are just a few left, their clothes hanging to dry a bright symbol of an ongoing tradition.

Two hours later we arrived at a table near the frigid-looking swimming pool. Gale introduced her husband and her shy children, who spoke a few words of English to us. Over mint tea we asked a few more pressing questions. *"Do you haggle for food in a shop or souk"?* No, you are quoted the correct price for food and either pay or it don't take the food. *"We've seen huge stacks of eggs being sold, how does anyone know if they're fresh?"* You smell them when you break them. Don't ever have a boiled egg here, as you can't tell if they're bad. Gale's husband, a quiet and gentle man, explained how their son was a chef, and how many years of tuition it took before you could be qualified. When we finally left the campsite we earnestly thanked Gale at the reception, she had taught us so much about the Moroccan way of life.

On hearing we were heading south to Zagora, Gale told us to look out for the Thursday market a couple of kilometres outside Agdz. As it happened, we needn't have been forewarned. Following the same pattern as markets further north, the intensity of human traffic told us something was taking place. Pulling onto rough ground next to another motorhome, we jumped out into the dust and looked around the walled enclosure. The souk wasn't like those we'd seen before. Hand-crafted clothes, fine leather and metal wares and piles of coloured spices were replaced here with less exotic, more useful things. Pots, teapots, work clothes and worn metal tools competed for attention with car tyres fashioned into water carriers and arch-shaped chequered donkey cushions and sheep. Almost everything was laid out directly on the dry rock-punched soil. One stall which had upgraded to a ground sheet held piles of what appeared to be rubbish; bits of old feathers, reptile parts and necklace beads; like ready-made potion concoctions; just add water.

In among the randomly ordered stalls, children ran, amid teetering mopeds and wandering donkeys, through the dusty wind and an air of chaos. An attempt to buy popcorn and nuts resulted in bemusement as everyone around Jay, including complete newcomers, were served while he was rendered invisible. Adopting a more forthright attitude, Jay thrust a guessed combination of coins forwards eventually resulting in a bag sized to match the value of metal. Walking through the market we took photographs where we dared. Our camera, which could easily have been worth the same amount as some people here earned in a year, seemed likely to cause offence as the most fascinating things were the faces of the people. Paying to photograph subjects felt wrong and resulted in false smiles, while sneaking shots from the hip felt underhand. We wondered how professional photographers manage the trick.

As we reached our vans the French-registered motorhome parked next to us was having a problem. An ill dog had sought shade underneath his van and refused to move. He didn't dare move for fear of hurting it. Charlie's treats came out, it didn't. Locals shouted at it, it did nothing. Starting the engine had no effect. A small crowd stood around, stumped, when it crawled out and flopped down next to the van of its own accord. A local grabbed it by its ruff and dragged it further away. Despite being dog lovers, we felt cold to the poor state of the wild dogs here. It simply felt like a different world to the cosseted Western European countries we normally inhabit. Either that or we were protecting ourselves from their misfortune. Other animals appeared well treated; only once did we see a young donkey driver beating his animal with a force we felt sickened by.

The caramelised peanuts we had bought at the souk were tucked into while watching the vista of the Draa valley unveil itself like a road movie. Although the sheer jaw-dropping drama of the earlier drive wasn't repeated, the mountains and decaying kasbahs rolled past us, eating up the miles to Zagora. At 100km, the Draa river is the longest in Morocco, snaking along the valley floor as we drew closer to the Sahara, we felt sure it must be lost in this desert.

We noticed a difference in the people around us, their skin was now darker, a much deeper tone than the olive-skinned Mediterranean faces of the north. Another change was the mode of transport, bicycles started to outnumber donkeys, perhaps it was harder to keep animals this far south. We passed a group of men walking along the side of the road. Some wore old coats and woolly hats. Others were in tatty overalls, each one of them with a battered and used spade, hoe or scythe. It struck us that we'd only really see men occupied in a tiny pool of occupations. These and many others worked in agriculture, tending to the land by hand or ploughing with the help of a donkey. Others worked in shops, bars and restaurants, where we'd seen very few women other than those in the large supermarkets or the western resort of Martil.

Finding Zagora wasn't difficult; there was only one road. Our expectations for the town were fairly low, after Ouarzazate, as it was another 'new' town built in the twentieth century. Flanked by the mountain after which it was named, Zagora was originally called *Tazagourt* the singular of plural *Tizigirt*, which is Berber for 'twin peaks', referring to the form the mountains took. Finding the campsite proved a little trickier. Shat-nav requested we *'take the next left'*, down a narrow, dusty pot-holed road. We glanced at each other and agreed this was another of her wacky short cuts. At the next, similar-looking road, the she became much more insistent *Turn left, now!*. So, in we went, bouncing along, minds being cast back to fuzzy TV images of war-torn Lebanon. Our doubts were assuaged by a couple of European faces walking in the other direction, and a battered hand-drawn sign with a cheery *'Camping Prends Ton Temp'* painted above an arrow.

Take Your Time Camping turned out to be an incredibly small packed-earth courtyard behind a tall metal gate. As we pulled in, halting at its smallness and wondering whether we were in the right place, a tall slim man sporting a gleaming smile and a thin blue robe strode out. He introduced himself as Abdula, told us to settle in and when we were ready walk through the archway to register. Once reversed into place the courtyard grew larger, enough for maybe five motorhomes. Through an archway stood a one story complex of rooms which could be rented. With a restaurant, bathrooms, decorations and colourful fabrics, it was an oasis compared with the conflict-zone look of the area outside.

Familiar mint teas, which Julie hated but always sipped at, were laid on as we sat in a Berber tent and completed the obligatory paperwork. Abdula clearly liked his gadgets, and liked to show them off. A laptop, iPod and brand new iPad made an appearance, incongruously flat shining surfaces on the cloth covered table. Back at Dave we plugged our mains electrical cable into a mud-splattered socket wedged at an angle into the earth wall.

In the early afternoon we investigated Zagora in an attempt to track down some alcohol. Finding a shop, ambitiously advertising itself as a supermarket, we grabbed a bottle of dusty orange cordial and some water and built up the courage to ask the owner where we might buy some beer. Without flinching or looking up he indicated behind him with his thumb *"Go to the hotel, you can get some there"*. At the reception desk of the hotel, the same question resulted in a quiet *"Through there"*, and a subtle gesture from the male receptionist. Feeling for all the world like like we were attempting some kind of back-street drug deal, we stepped through two small rooms, the curtains all closed. Behind a set of tall wooden screens, in the half darkness of a final room, we walked into another side of Morocco.

The air in this final room was thick with tobacco smoke. Men huddled in small groups around low tables topped with small bottles of beer, all the same brand, with no glasses. It seemed we'd found the only local's bar in the city. Julie saw several heads turn as she walked in, quite clearly the only woman in there. It felt seedy and a little bit threatening, but no one bothered us. The grumpy barman asked what we wanted. Julie asked what wine he had. He pointed past her around the screens we had come through. Peering at a small side room we understood; wine was for take-out only. Stacked up behind the bar were crates of beer, two types. We ordered one each and sat down at one of the few empty tables.

As we spoke in hushed tones to each other, this wasn't a raised voice place. Looking around we saw that we were drinking much faster than the locals. At about £1.50 for a 33cl can, it was a reasonable price to us, so probably an expensive luxury to them. In a rush to escape the dour barman, we'd somehow ordered a different beer to everyone else. Jay got the attention of a man sat next to him, sporting a copied motorbike jacket, he explained to us that there was actually no difference between the beers; the bar only sold one type of drink, which was brewed in Morocco.

After a couple of beers the place wasn't feeling any more welcoming so we opted for some take out wine. The door to the small room was locked, so we explained at the bar that we'd like to buy some wine, quickly a man appeared with keys and opened it. The tiny room had a few different types of wine, all Moroccan, and a price list on the back of the door. After some debate we bought a couple of bottles of red wine for about £6 each, and topped our illicit purchases off with a few cans of beer. Julie stood alone with the bags while payment was being made, two men walked in, nodded and smiled at her. She said they were probably pitying the poor European woman who couldn't live without alcohol!

Alcohol securely wrapped in newspaper and hidden in opaque carrier bags, Chris remembered he'd promised to get meat while we were out. So far we'd avoided this particular challenge, but the beers, and our achievement in procuring them, helped to summon up the courage to tackle it head on. The small butchers only had space for the butcher behind its counter, which was an open window out into the street. Our eyes were all drawn to a huge leg of something hanging, exposed to the elements outside. With a combination of French and mime, we managed to convey the rather obvious fact we wanted some meat and the butcher grabbed the leg and hacked a chunk off it, dicing it before handing it over. Unaware of what we'd bought, and feeling a little euphoric, we triumphantly returned to the campsite. As we ate the meat later, this euphoria maybe explained how Jay and Chris managed to drink the newly acquired alcohol stash, laughing and joking their way into the small hours of the morning. Waking worse for wear, Julie produced a small piece of paper recording the decision they'd reached the previous evening to buy a goat, with Chris acting as *Chief Ne'goat'iator*.

With both drivers in too sorry a state to do any driving, we settled in for another day in Zagora. Abdula stopped by and pointed out that Dave's leaf springs were sagging and Christina, being much newer than Dave, could do with an extra one or two for better ground clearance. Amazingly he had a cousin who would be stopping by later who could fix them. Politely declining, we smiled and thanked him, lending him a can of WD40 to oil his moped chain with, as a peace offering. The mopeds, which all conform to pretty much the same design, cost around £1400 new, a huge expense for most Moroccans. Abdula's had covered 22,000Km before the odometer cable snapped some time ago.

The day was spent recovering, fending off urchins in the campsite, dog walking and sorting many megabytes of photographs. Jay tracked down the famous painted sign depicting a camel train, with an arrow pointing off down the road stating '52 days to Timbuktu', and we all replicated a pose by epic traveller Michael Palin on one of his long journeys in Africa. In the evening Abdula's low ceilinged, chilly restaurant welcomed us with tagines and cold chips. His iPad made a reappearance to record an impromptu band performance, its most impressive member a hulk of a man playing a twelve-stringed instrument and singing. A Moroccan seated next to Jay clapped along, telling us how he was here on holiday from his job at the brewery in Marrakech. It seemed he liked to take his work with him, as his French was tinged with a familiar beer-induced twang.

MOVIE MAGIC

After five hours of driving north through undiminished scenery, we found ourselves back in Ouarzazate, parked alongside Peter and Jill who we'd briefly met in Zagora. With a backdrop of their motorhome shining white in the early afternoon sun, we stood aghast as Peter nonchalantly told us how he and Jill had once found themselves stuck on the streets amid groups of rival rioters during a there-and-back tour of the length of Africa. *"It wasn't really a problem, they weren't interested in us Europeans"* he shrugged, telling us immediately afterwards how they'd picked up a badly beaten German backpacker and helped him back to their guarded campsite. Travelling Morocco was, for them, clearly no more challenging than driving to the British seaside for a weekend away. We were impressed.

Taking to the streets of Ouarzazate again we asked around for the only supermarket as we'd heard it sold beer and wine. Finding it was both a disappointment and a small victory. We were pleased to have sussed out where it was, an ordinary-looking shop front with little to set it apart from its neighbours. We were less pleased with the false-European nature of it; tired sparse isles like a 1950's corner shop, inflated prices stuck onto faded labels. Picking up a few bits and bobs, the act of buying alcohol required almost begging the shadowy figure behind a counter for a few cans of beer. Pricing was by the shelf, rather than the brand. Eager to escape the down-the nose sneer from the man tasked with touching the filthy beer, Chris and Jay didn't find out what they'd actually bought until back in the confines of the campsite - cans of Flag and Casablanca, both lagers and being the cheapest, were brewed by *Societe des Brasseries du Maroc*, the only Moroccan beer brewer.

A second task needed tackling; we needed to buy more meat - a chicken and some mince. Stories from fellow travellers who ask for a chicken, which was subsequently strangled, plucked, cleaned and hacked up in front of their eyes, meant Julie was less than keen to witness this spectacle and was chuffed to discover pre-killed chickens being sold, which just required hacking up with a machete. The mince seller had more fun with us. As we pointed at the mince, gesturing how much we wanted, he announced a price of *forty*. We assumed Dirhams, so about £4, seemed reasonable. He then added *Euros*, with a straight face. By this point the bag of mince was about to find its way into one of our backpacks and was rapidly retrieved. Seeing this he smiled, waved a hand at us and pointed to an A4 sheet of yellowing paper behind him. It was a price list, and mince, *hache,* was 80Dh a Kg, we'd had about half a kilo. We didn't know whether he'd have actually taken nearly ten times the price from us, but he went on to say that all butchers have this standard price list, ensuring none of his fellow meat-manglers would have the same chance to have a laugh at our expense.

With little to hold us in Ouarzazate, and the prospect of a nerve-racking trip over the mountains to Marrakech to come, we left early the next day. Just outside Ouarzazate lies the Atlas Film Studio, the largest in the world due to the fact most of it is nothingness, desert and mountains drifting off endlessly. Over the past forty or fifty years, as technically Lawrence of Arabia was filmed here before the studio was built, Hollywood, the BBC and others have taken advantage of the crystal clear light, good weather and cheap labour. Our guide, a young and easy going chap who proclaimed himself to be named Bob, reeled off the list of productions as he walked: Black Hawk Down, The Mummy, Star Wars, Gladiator, The Living Daylights and more.

We'd looked the studio up before visiting and found it had a mixed reputation. The poor reviews seemed mainly focussed around the dilapidated state of the sets, abandoned with little maintenance as soon as the filming was complete. Sure enough, the full size, mocked-up F16 fighter from Romancing the Stone, which welcomed us at the gate, appeared ready to puff into dust, after over 25 years sitting about unloved. We didn't care - Bob was a natural entertainer, full of interesting facts and we all bounced off each other, the only people in the studio.

In among the false, decaying worlds, the magic of the movies became real. Hollywood would design the sets, and they'd be fashioned locally under the guidance of imported craftsmen. The result was incredible. Even where the years had worn away at the paint, or the lack of high definition cameras had warranted little detail, the sets looked real. Reaching out to touch the sandstone walls of the Gladiator slave market, the sensation of painted polystyrene was genuinely unexpected. Jay unleashed his rendition of Russell Crowe's Maximus Decimus Meridius 'Commander of the armies of the North' speech, confirming his place in history as a failed amateur actor.

Mud kasbahs with winding passages, a stalled souk, a dark imposing Buddhist temple, Jerusalem moulded around Jesus' house and the Luxor palace had us all laughing and playing in their sheer scale and unusualness. Bob helped us fool around on the sets, pointing out clever camera positions to capture us kissing a Sphinx, leaning on a pyramid or a tiny versions of Jay stood on Julie's hand. The hour flew. Outside the studio, under the glazed stare of a row of enormous mummies, the map came out. We'd decided to head to another famous movie location for the night before tackling the Tizi-n-Tichka pass to Marrakech. Âit-Benhaddou, a hillside fortified town and UNESCO World Heritage site, stood further to the north, a few kilometres from the main road.

In our convoy we were often passed by lorries, their overloaded state now rendered normal to us by just our few days travelling the country. Being overtaken by hovering sheep raised our eyebrows, and a few chuckles, as they bumbled past in a makeshift enclosure welded to the top of an ancient pale-blue transit van. Following the unfortunate airborne beasts for a while, they struggled over one another, shifting around in the space-less pen until the van lurched into a space in front of a shop and we waved them goodbye.

Turning north from the main road, the tarmac was again eaten away at the sides, the route becoming a single track bordered by gravel. As taxis and coaches approached, everyone slowed to a crawl, took to the gravel and crawled past one another. It made for slow progress, but felt quite safe in the bright light of the cloudless day. The road swept alongside the Ounila river, waterless in the near-dead rock-strewn rolling hills and plains. Ranks of beautifully fired green, yellow, red and blue round plates shone at us from each pulling in place, their purveyors hidden among the rocks.

Rounding a corner, Âit-Benhaddou the fortified city, or *ksar*, grew up before us in a tumbling mass of mud walls and towers, drawing our stares and threatening to distract us off the winding road. Tired from driving we passed the vantage point and pulled into a parking area marked out with a this-way-to-the-ksar sign. Before Dave's wheels had straightened a man confidently waved us into a corner of the parking area, we followed his direction, a little suspicious as always. We soon realised this wasn't the official parking, but the difference between official and unofficial in Morocco is often a slight one. The man owned the restaurant next to where we were parked, and sealed the deal with the offer of electricity. Having only one socket, Chris and Tina's cable found itself disappearing through a small window to be plugged into a socket inside someone's house.

We were all hungry. Walking the single street town, with more streets marked out in a grid, but never actually made, it appeared to owe its entire existence to the ksar. Although once fully inhabited, only a few families still live in the crumbling mud structure, favouring the featureless but resilient, and electrically connected, concrete cubes in the town. Fortified with hot chips and omelette we headed for the ksar, hardening ourselves for a gauntlet of guides we'd need to fend off. Our first obstacle was an ingenious *tat-funnel*, a narrowing cobbled street which forced visitors past a series of local souvenir shops. Perhaps our physical state, washing less than we should and sporting worn walking boots, earned us an easier time with the sellers, they hardly spoke to us, just the odd joking *buy-no-look?* parody of their countrymen's *look-no-buy?* battle cry.

The approach to the ksar is across the Ounila river. Although its bed is perhaps fifty meters wide, only a sliver is wet, the rest an array of boulders laying motionless awaiting the next flood. Sandbags stacked two by two form a series of easily navigated stepping stones, over the wet, ensuring everyone crosses at the same point, right into the jaws of the faux-guides. One of them broke away from the group and followed us as far as the entrance gate. By now we had all experienced a near knowledge-less guide forcing themselves upon us, and perhaps it showed on our faces as we waved him off, *la shukran,* no thanks. Women inside the ksar who attempted to invite us in to their homes got the same response, their faces making no attempt to hide a flash of contempt when we declined. We knew they'd want to be paid.

The ksar has no electricity, rooms and corridors were in near darkness. Without a guide we relaxed, taking our time to imagine what it may have been like to live there. Working our way upwards through narrow alleys and stairways, we found a shop selling simple but beautiful paintings made by painting paper with tea, henna and saffron, and then heating it gently over a gas flame. It reminded Jay of the opening scenes from the film The English Patient, where a brush plays across paper, recreating a cave drawing of hunting people. Jay attempted to haggle for one of the paintings, but walked away empty handed. The seller, whose photograph showed him as an extra in *Gladiator*, made a single concession on the price, which unusually was advertised, and no more.

Climbing higher we walked past houses crowded together, some modest, others resembling small urban castles. Among the buildings sheep pens and stables, a market place, silos and lofts. At the top of the ksar we looked down over the rooftops, some almost crumbling as we watched, others with tall decorated towers. Several parts of the ksar looked freshly repaired, Hollywood often used it as a replacement for Jerusalem and would pay for it to be patched up as needed.

High above the town on the top of the hill stood another cubed earth building, a loft-fortress. Linked to the town by a fortified stairway this fortress was the village's last bastion of resistance in the event of a siege. The view from the top was incredible, looking down over the river valley and across to the snow-capped mountains. We sat like high-up gods, watching tiny people and animals working in the fields far below us. A couple of apparently inebriated, jolly and foolish Moroccans joined us, sitting in amongst the rocks and staring out into the vista.

Working our way back down through the ksar we met with Sasha and Andy who were touring Morocco by hire car, stopping in accommodation ranging from riads to campsites. It sounded like a great way to see the country without a motorhome. Having paid for a guide on their way in, they pointed out where the scenes from the film Gladiator were shot, including a large flat circular area that had been transformed into an amphitheatre. We stopped off in the hotel at the end of *tat-funnel* for a warming mint tea, and as we found a table overlooking the ksar, beautifully lit by the setting sun, we heard two familiar voices, Roger and Sandy who had been on Gale's tour of the Kasbah in Agdz were just settling in with a beer.

That evening the eight travelling Brits shared stories and life lessons, and as the night outside grew dark more beer cans stood hollow on our table. Each round had to be practically wrung out of the ever disappearing waiter who seemed aghast we were drinking more than a single can each. We walked out practically sober, craning our necks upwards at the vivid stars. Sasha and Andy headed back to their room, while Roger and Sandy's heater-less motorhome was parked up next to Dave and Christina. We hoped our new neighbours would survive the night.

MARRAKECH MADNESS

Mountain passes draw out our emotions. Fear being the overriding one. Fear of falling rocks, sections too steep to climb, snow, ice, landslides, all cross our minds before we attempt one. On the flip side, we feel elation at overcoming the unease and finding ourselves driving through some of the most incredible scenery. The Tizi-n-Tichka pass didn't fail us, on either the fear or elation perspective!

We'd always known the city we were going to as Marrakesh, but the road signs we passed and our map call it Marrakech. Until a few decades ago, the whole of Morocco was widely known as the *Kingdom of Marrakech*, and in many languages the country is still known as *Marrakech* today. Regardless of spelling, this was one city Shat-nav could find, but she couldn't make up her mind how long it would take us to get there. The evening before she had decided six and half hours would do it, which sounded tortuous. The next day she changed her mind to three and a half hours, maybe she actually was clever enough to work out it was faster in daylight. From experience we figured on five hours. Initially setting off in the wrong direction, we headed south, Bob at the movie studio had advised us against taking a motorhome along the more direct route north, as it was more of a track than a road. With hours of driving still to come, we didn't feel gung-ho enough to take our, by-now complaining, squeaking suspension over ten kilometres of rubble.

Settling back onto the main road, with Chris and Tina following on behind, we turned north and headed for the snow-capped peaks in the distance. Endless roadside sellers marked this out as a popular tourist route, even in the middle of winter, with long stalls of coloured pots and fossils. As ever, apart from the goods themselves, no marketing was done. None of the European style signs, flags or sellers antics marked out one plot from another as we drove past.

Gradually the rugged sides to the road lifted upwards, and patches of the much-feared white stuff clung onto shadowed sections of the hills. The road itself proved smooth, a beloved white line sectioning it into two broadish lanes, and protection from the steep side drop-offs with crenelated blocks of concrete. Red and yellow painted girders had been hammered into the road edge, the normal method of signalling where a snow-bound driver might find the route when it seriously bad weather. At the last of the main towns, sitting idle in a car park, lorries fitted with ploughs had our hearts thumping.

Settling into a rhythm along the quiet road, we pulled in a few times to stretch, breathe in the air and the view. As Jay laid flat out on a protective roadside wall easing shoulder pain from the concentration, Julie found herself fending off begging children. Once again surprising us by appearing in a most inhospitable, remote place, they demanded the lip salve she was applying. We'd grown used to constantly saying no, but we hadn't become comfortable with it. As a European visiting a country like Morocco, we found the incessant begging is something you simply have to live with, whether you choose to give or not.

Climbing higher, we would catch up with laden lorries on the steeper sections, their hazard warning lights indicating their almost complete lack of movement. It would usually be a fairly simple process to move past them, as the road could often be seen winding along a contour around a broad section of hillside. In a right hand drive vehicle, overtaking was trickier for Chris, once we'd passed the obstacle we used the walkie-talkies to let him know when the road was clear for him to follow. Our left hand drive position proved to be no advantage overtaking a lorry which changed gear and started to accelerate. We were left exposed, sat alongside the lorry as the road surface narrowed and a previously unseen group of women and children appeared on the far side of the road. We had the choice of braking and trying to fit back in between Chris and the lorry, or speeding up to get past. His left wheels thumping along the rough edge of the road Dave gave it everything he had, squeezing us in front of the lorry just before we reached the group. That manoeuvre was perhaps the most dangerous thing to happen to us in Morocco, and was purely our fault.

Reaching the top we stopped and took in the view, before slowly making our way down the other side, engine braking as much as possible to protect our warming brake pads. Our eyebrows raised as we looked down on the road ahead, the pass ran across a narrow ridge, the roadside steeply dropping off to the left and right. It seemed impossible that the tarmac could cling to this edge of rock, but as we made our way down towards it our fears were allayed as the optical illusion revealed itself, it was much wider in real life.

In among the mountains proper, there are no places to stop and sleep. Any flat area off the road has been commandeered by a shop, its rear wall often hanging out over a precipitous drop. This lack of halting opportunity was perhaps a good thing for Chris, who has a fear of heights. For the life of us we couldn't work out how he'd built the courage to take on this drive, but he never faltered as we slowly descended through packs of hairpin bends, edged with sheer drops.

As we swung down off the pass, the traffic increased. Knee high, painted white, concrete markers at the side of the road counted us down towards Marrakech, their red tops indicating the type of road we were on. We tried as a rule to only go on roads with these markers. While they range from narrow and pot-holed to beautifully flat wide tarmac, you generally know you'll be able to get a motorhome through them. Coming over the pass we'd seen a group of women carrying huge bundles of hay on their backs, here horses pulled carts stacked unfeasibly high with it. Lorries once again sported huge *afro* style hair-dos of goods wrapped under tarpaulins, and donkeys took up their place against the road edge again. It had taken us four and a half hours to tackle the snaking ribbon of tarmac.

Turning at the signpost for our campsite and made our way slowly along a couple of kilometres of dirt track, winding through a small residential area. Numerous signposts reassuring us that we were still on the right path as we rumbled off into nowhere. Groups of children ran towards the vans, hands out, demanding bonbons. Exhausted, we ignored them and carried on slowly. Reaching the campsite gates, they opened to welcome us into another oasis of calm, only this one was the most incredible sight among the dust and deprivation outside. Twenty or so motorhome pitches spaced out in a circle around the outside of the ornate and brand new central buildings. Tall grasses and trees separated the gravel-floored parking places. A glimpse of a pale blue, overflowing infinity swimming pool had us pointing and gibbering. We parked on pitches next to each other, a strip of grass and a couple of heavily laden olive trees between us. Metalwork lanterns were placed at intervals to light the site at night. Berber style tents topped off the authentic, if unexpected opulence.

We were taken on a tour by Pascale, who was French and who, along with her husband André, owned the campsite and had built it from an olive field. As we walked the stress of the drive melted away. Tree lined terracing either side of the shimmering infinity pool sported sun loungers covered in plump cushions and beds to snooze away a hot afternoon in the shade. The toilets and showers, lined with dark slate tiles, looked like something from a five star hotel, as did the restaurant with its glass-walled wine cellar. The small snug area had huge leather sofas to sink into and a vast solid wood coffee table next to the open fireplace, all sitting under a hand-carved ceiling that had taken two men six weeks to complete. Our overflowing laundry could be taken from us, washed, dried, folded and returned and we could arrange morning delivery to our van doors of freshly baked, warm croissants or pain-au-chocolate. We had found motorhome nirvana!

At five thirty the next morning, the ever-present excitement of being in Morocco woke Jay, who used the early hours to watch Gladiator and seek out the scenes we'd visited the day before. Bang on time at 8:30, warm and soft pastries appeared, left quietly on a tray outside the van, warm chocolate filling oozed out of them, these were clearly not Moroccan style pastries. We hungrily ate them before spending an age under the drencher showers, scrubbing away at the desert dust. The campsite was heaven, only the heaven was a long way from anywhere, Marrakech was miles away. No problem though as we'd already arranged with Pascale for a taxi into town and back later in the day.

Walking Charlie and Loli outside the campsite grounds, a pack of wild dogs took an interest. The trick of simply picking something up, or even pretending to pick something up, saw them scatter off into the surrounding olive trees. Comparing the mud-floored fields of trees with the campsite provided a fabulous view of the contrast, and the work that the owners had invested in the place. Sitting outside our vans in the sunshine we talked about it again trying to work out how they could possibly get their investment back. On the surface it seemed like another Walt Disney Camping investment where it could never pay off.

At 1pm, the dogs left to snooze in their respective vans, we climbed eagerly into a well used Land Rover, branded with campsite advertising. Its snorkel, roof rack containing petrol canisters and spare tyres told of its main role in life, taking tourists onto the sand dunes near Zagora. Considering it was a sturdy 4x4 the driver still took his time along the dirt road to the campsite, not wanting to bounce his passengers around too much. No children ran to us now asking for sweets.

Out on the main roads, a degree of chaos ensued. Cars darted from lane to lane, and new lanes were created from nothing more than a need to get past. Traffic took on a life of its own, a flowing mass, with little apparent order. The feeling of relief was evident on Chris and Jay's faces; being chauffeured suited them just fine! We were dropped us off by the *Koutoubia* mosque, the driver confident we'd be able to navigate our way around Morocco's third largest city and back to the mosque's minaret, standing tall to one end of the town's famous market square, *Djemaa el Fna*.

Like many Moroccan cities, Marrakech is made up of both an old fortified city (the medina) and modern neighbourhoods, usually built by the French. The open square of Djemaa el Fna is the biggest in continental Africa and possibly one of the busiest in the world. Edged along one side by traditional souks catering for locals and tourists alike, the other sides house hotels and cafés with terraces for viewing the scene below, it was to one of these that we headed first to get our bearings.

Climbing the narrow wooden stairs up to the first level terrace we found ourselves a table overlooking the square. From here we could stare down from above, watching the bustling activity and taking surreptitious photographs. Most of the miniature figures in the square were obviously western tourists, but a few locals walked among them, carrying thin plastic bags containing fruit or bread. The stalls on the edge of the souk had green awnings pulled down low to provide shade.

In the middle of the square a cluster of stalls offered to juice fresh oranges for thirsty visitors, their sides wearing unravelled orange peel like hair. Large parasols were dotted around the square, sellers squatting on the floor in the pool of shadow below, their eyes lazily watching their stock of souvenirs, wicker baskets, leather bags and even baby turtles. Women sat in small groups offering henna tattoos and a man wandered around with a full-length mirror, offering it for sale. On the other side of the orange juice stalls, men with Barbary apes on chains or snakes proffered them to passing tourists as a photo opportunity.

The show played out below, keeping us entertained but with a niggling sense of unease. Fes and Marrakech compete for the tourist dollar, both offering a sense of the ancient. Our view of Fes was undoubtedly coloured by the shielding influence of an official guide. We wondered if the playful edge we'd experienced in our dealings with Moroccan sellers across the country existed here. During our walk across the square Julie had already had her hand pulled out of her pocket by a woman insistent about applying a henna tattoo onto it. But there were four of us now, strength in numbers, and since the guidebooks didn't describe Marrakech as being as disorientating as they had Fes, we chose to tackle the city alone.

As we mused, we caught the eye of our waiter and asked to pay for our teas. He took our Dirhams, explaining he didn't have the 5Dh change but he would go and get it. He failed to reappear, so we decided we would fail to leave, certain of a minor scam being played out. Eventually we spotted the same waiter serving someone else among a small throng of his colleagues, and Tina made it clear we were waiting for change. He immediately produced the money, which would have been his tip, and we left, shaking our heads.

Stepping back into the square we had no destination but the souk, so we turned left under the covered slats and wandered rather than marched. Our gait appeared to mark us out as much as our cleanliness and clothing. Harassing calls and whistles chimed from each and every shop. In itself, the calling was something we'd become comfortable with, but here it had a hard edge to it and took on an aggressive feel, tiring.

Wooden slats covered the walkways giving a Venetian blind effect to the light. Jars of olives stacked high on some stalls, others were a sea of colour from hanging scarves. Silver mint tea sets, ornate lamps, leather slippers and carpets filled the stalls, it was just like all the other souks in terms of merchandise, only here there were many *No Photography* signs, in scrawled English.

Our noses led us to an area where stalls cooked fish and chips, much like those in the Chefchaouen market. Spotting a stall with a makeshift table and small plastic stools free we ordered fish and chips each and sat down to eat. The food came in waves as it was ready, and with a bit of prompting for things that were missing we built up a portion each. Locals flickered looks showed surprise, we were the only tourists eating here, perhaps all the others ate in the restaurants surrounding the square. Cats curled themselves around our feet as we ate, rewarded with bits of fish skin. Behind us, youths with seemingly nothing better to do leant on an old fridge watching us.

Finishing our meal we asked the man cooking up the food how much we needed to pay. *"Twenty,"* he replied and after a pause *"each"*. The price seemed reasonable, we'd just paid more than that for drinks in the café, so we handed over the Dirhams and left. Away from the stall Tina quietly told us another man had leaned in and whispered to the owner after he had given us the total, twenty, telling him to charge us that much each. Only she had seen the crinkled smiles as we paid four times the local rate, confirmed by the unusual presence of signs with costs at other stalls. Of course, our wallets could easily afford the additional few pounds, but the feeling of being cheated was sour. We notched it up to experience.

Not having a guide gave us the freedom to get lost around the souks and we happily wandered around with nowhere specific to go. Coming across a photography museum we spent some time in the calmness looking at images of old Marrakech, there was very little difference to the images of today, only a lack of colour. Sitting on the roof terrace of the museum we looked out over the satellite dishes and minarets towards the High Atlas Mountains that we'd conquered just a couple of days before. Shrouded in mist we could just make out the white snow-capped peaks rising high above the city.

Wandering around the back streets, away from the bustle of the souk, we found a shop selling black Hammam soap. It was in plain plastic tubs and a fraction of the price being charged a hundred metres away in the main souk. The lack of no photography signs gave us an opportunity, so while Tina distracted the stall owner trying on several bracelets, we took photos of the tiny scrabbling turtles for sale. These shops sold to locals, not the tourists. Tired old shoes and rusty sewing machines sat near an ancient petrol pump used to fuel the million-and-one mopeds charging around.

By now we were quite lost and forgetting about our directional misfortune in Ouarzazate, we stopped and asked a policeman the way. *"To where?"* he rather obviously asked. Having forgotten the name of the square, some comedy miming got the message across, *the big square*. He smiled, pointed up a back street and walked off back to his duties. We could tell his directions were good as almost immediately the goods in the shops got newer, as hotels and riads started to line the streets. Turning a corner we were back in the square, the entrance walkway now lined with old robed men, most of them clutching a walking stick, all sitting, staring straight ahead, silent.

Djemaa el Fna has a reputation for changing character at night, coming to life. Our taxi was collecting us a couple of hours after dark so we could experience it. As the sun set behind the minaret, shadows crept across the square. Thick groups of locals gathered around story tellers, acrobats and musicians. Raising a camera above one group to snap the capering men in the centre, Jay found himself face-to-face with an unsmiling clown, hand thrust out demanding money. A few coins failed to pacify him, so Jay turned away and walked off, the performer returned to his audience.

Chris played along when he was approached by a man with a snake. The tiny thing, not much more than a worm was draped across a shoulder. Chris jokingly complained that it wasn't a real snake, he wanted a bigger one if he was to have his photograph taken. Becoming a magnet for all sized snakes, within a few seconds he had three draped around his neck, their owners stood beside holding them, a fixed stare into the camera as Tina captured the moment. Offering a few pounds as payment, the men refused, demanding around £30. Chris' response to this was, in retrospect, perfect as he loudly and angrily stated they were conmen, thieves and he would pay them nothing, fending off their grabbing hands he strode away. The men hissed and shouted obscenities, but Chris had succeeding in attracting much attention and so they didn't pursue him. With zero police presence in the square, we found Marrakech a heavily frequented tourist trap. Far more intimidating than the small towns and villages we'd grown to love across the country, we doubted we would ever return to this city.

To cool off we took ourselves to the juice sellers, and watched as oranges were split and then held on top of a spinning machine to squeeze every last drop of juice from them. After much negotiation Tina found her boots being shined by the most persistent shoe-shiner, in the world, who had also offered to shine trainers, and suede. His shaking, gnarled hands indicated fabulous acting or a medical condition, in either case he did a great job and earned a tip.

As the sun finally set on the square, the open space began to fill with wheeled and numbered food stalls. Arranged in rows, they competed with one another to generate the most smoke, pumping out clouds of the stuff, fogging the glow of strings of electric lights. White-hatted and coated touts bouncing around their affiliated stall, latching onto us, quickly working out we were British and swamping us with their catch-phrases. *"117 takes you to heaven"*, *"not 118, they're too late"*, *"luverly juberlee food"*, *"You know Jamie Oliver, he's my brother"*. Circling the stalls twice, hearing all the catch phrases, number 65 won out, mainly as it had a free table! The colourful array of skewered meats, sea food and vegetables sitting uncooled, threatened to give us serious cause to regret eating them, but we did anyway. As we ate, groups of beggars worked the tables, mainly women and children. Some sold packs of tissues, others stole food from our table as we posed for a photo with the staff. The chips turned out to be cold, disappointing Julie and Tina yet again. With a final look back across the square, alive with swarms of people we headed to meet our taxi and return with relief to our campsite.

We did nothing the following day, but relax and recover. At 8:30am warm pain-au-chocolat were brought to us by Pascale, who seemed to do most of the jobs on the site, while Andre ran the desert tours side of things. She asked Jay how we'd enjoyed Marrakech, earning a scathing response, and simply smiled back with an enigmatic *"hmm, yes"*. In the evening we enjoyed a delayed valentines meal, as it was now the 15th February, in Pascale and Andrés self designed restaurant. To our right the still infinity pool reflected up-lit palm trees, to our left André's glass walled wine cellar, from where he produced bottles of perfectly chilled local *Vin Gris,* grey wine, which is actually very pale pink, to wash down the amazing French food cooked for us by Pascale.

Once we'd eaten, the offer of a fire tempted us into the snug where André got the wood fire going. The smell of burning wood and the wine chilled us out. Inhibitions gone we soon began to interrogate André, who was originally from Belgium, about how he could afford to build a place as grand as this, gesturing at the stucco ceiling above. He told us how he used to run a company which dealt with Moroccan mining companies; silver, phosphorous, and some others. He sold it, and after he and Pascale travelled for a while, adopting three children from Brazil along the way, they finally bought an olive tree grove and set about designing the campsite. They only paid a Moroccan architect to sign-off the designs. It all sounded incredible. While none of us could fathom how he would ever turn a profit from the place, we guessed their efforts were entirely devoted to their children's futures.

The questions carried on late into the night, Pascale taking over from André as the night wore on and we added more wood to the fire. Between them they explained to us how tricky it was running a business in Morocco, requiring stacks of paperwork, especially to get a liquor licence. The import tax for bringing goods into the country is 40% and VAT is a further 20%, so the motorhome parts that they sold were only ever emergency-only purchases. With the tax figure in mind, it was also a good job they couldn't get an import licence for alcohol or that would be prohibitively expensive too. Instead they sold only local wine, but only the best of it. Finally as the night was ending they told us the problems they had with the local staff who would randomly quit no matter how much you paid them, or what sort of contract you had with them. If Allah willed someone not to go to work, they wouldn't turn up. *Insha'Allah,* meaning *God willing,* was the phrase used to explain why anything not intended to happen, happened.

COASTING HOME

After a few days of relaxing in luxury, the road called again. Chris was keen to tackle the Tizi-n-Test pass to Agadir, indicated on our map with a series of ant-like back dots on a zigzagging yellow road. *Difficult or dangerous section of road* read the key, which made him all the more determined to try it. Photographs of the road on the internet showed it looking passable, but we were already a long way south and time was ticking away on our month-long motorhome insurance. A few days would be needed to travel back to Tangier, so we opted to take the road west to the Atlantic, to the chilled-out resort of Essaouira. A disappointed Chris agreed to join us on the easy route.

Driving the outskirts of Marrakech provided nerve-wracking fun. Lane markings were ignored as two lanes became three at traffic lights. Mopeds anticipated the green light rather than waiting for it. Buses pulled out without warning and cars would materialise from nowhere at right-angles to the rest of the traffic flow. Taking it slowly and employing an un-British attitude of using the horn worked a treat and we entered the Marjane supermarket car park unharmed. As we left, our empty cupboards were only partially restocked, enough to last us the few days back to Spain and low-cost Lidl. Our wine stash was more substantially replenished, including a couple of bottles of the grey wine we'd been served by André.

The landscape heading towards the coast was fairly featureless and the rough road soon turned into a smooth, straight dual carriageway of tarmac, bliss. Between towns we managed to get up to 100kph for the first time in weeks. As the sun slowly cooked us in Dave's cab, a virtual line was drawn across the land, our surroundings changed from dirt brown to lush green. Fields accommodated sheep, as opposed to goats munching on the grass verges beside the road and as we neared the coastal resort of Essaouira, it felt like we were drawing closer to Europe.

At the campsite we pulled into spaces next to each other, the campsite owner promptly gesticulating at us to move closer to our neighbour and each other. Space was at a premium, the place was packed with motorhomes and a couple of bikers in tents. With our vans in a place the owner was happy with, we went for a walk along the road, or more specifically the roadworks. The pavement stretching from the campsite into the town was dug up, piles of displaced block paving stood untouched, the odd brick falling from its group and breaking. Fed up of scrabbling over bricks and potholes, we climbed the scrubby dunes to reach the beach.

Sitting high up on a log, we watched couples taking camel rides along the sand to some ruins at the far end of the beach. Stretching away to our right buildings three or four storeys high lined the beach leading to a fortress. In front of us a long, low island containing a wildlife sanctuary blocked our view of the Atlantic as it reached for the horizon. Weary from the day's drive we headed back to the vans for dinner. Again Chris and Jay managed to put a serious dent in the recently acquired wine stash, this time thoughtfully moving themselves outside as it became clear they were no longer coherent to the ladies. Lighting a fire they sat and chatted into the wee small hours, much to the pleasure of the bikers sleeping three feet away from them in their tents.

A morning visitor to the campsite was selling fish, fresh from the port. Chris and Jay haggled with him for four large red snapper fish until they settled on a price they were happy with (around £2 per fish). It was a more than we'd have paid in the port, but it meant the fish could be put straight into our fridge once the man had gutted them for us. Jay, stood among a squadron of mewing cats, watching the process to learn how to do it.

The makings of an evening BBQ arranged, we all set off to explore the city of Essaouira, also known since the sixteenth century by its Portuguese name of Mogador. Centuries old battlements complete with cannons mounted along the crenelated walls face the sea and port, south of which a wide, clean beach stretches for two miles, our path into the city. We made our way past the rather lacklustre touts trying to sell camel rides to the ruins, a fortification from the Portuguese occupation. Further up the beach a woman showed some Marrakech spirit by walking a good two hundred meters to offer us knitted hats, but otherwise everything was fairly laid back.

We passed a local school group, heading to the water's edge for surfing lessons. Further along, the beach came alive with the shouts and grunts of groups of lads playing football on pitches marked out in the sand. One 'pitch' had goal posts where as others settled for the universal alternative; a heap of clothing. Footwear ranging from barefoot or flip flops to studded boots was accompanied by an array of European football club shirts, t-shirts or bare chests. While we couldn't work it out, we were sure they knew who was on which side. Charlie took a passing interest in the ball but the lure of dead crabs washed up by the sea was, as always, stronger.

Away from the football people sunbathed, children played in the sand, jeans and shorts replacing the Djellaba as the standard outfit. Walking up the steps towards the town we saw our first lookie-lookie men, walking around with armfuls of bags, sunglasses and watches, all the latest designer names of course, and all very poor imitations. An odd beggar sat in the shade, arm outstretched, mumbling as we passed, but there was no hassle, life here was seriously chilled.

Essaouira, the Berber name for the city, means *the wall*, a reference to the fortress which encloses it. Walking around its walls we reached the small but frenetic harbour. Bustling with life, this was where all the locals were engaged in graft. Weathered men unloaded battered old fishing boats, the daily catch either being packed straight into Lego-like coloured boxes of ice and sent off in trucks, or laid out on flattened cardboard boxes and tables for passers-by to purchase. Eels, huge spider crabs, rays and hundreds of sardines lay freshly dead awaiting purchase and cooking. Locals walked around with carrier bags brimming with staring eyes and silvery skin. Charlie had entered a heaven of sniffs, happily snuffling out the best bits of discarded fish, at one point scoring a full sardine, and jealously guarding it when we made a half-hearted attempt to relive him of it.

An entire coast of seagulls swooped around the sky above the harbour, or waited, perched up high, for their moment to dive in and grab sustenance. Gnarl-handed men stood absent-mindedly tying vicious hook after vicious hook onto a myriad of lines. Above them, shouts accompanied the noise of hammering and welding as old boats were repaired on stands overlooking the waterside circus. Jay and Chris took the opportunity to top up the evenings BBQ with a plastic bag full of sardines. The weather was hot and we had a day of sightseeing ahead of us, so Jay scrapped a few handfuls of ice into the bag which had fallen from the back of a lorry, literally. Walking along the beach later two men separately pointed at the melting ice in the bag, the second taking a pencil and poking holes to drain the smelly water. *"Bad water"* he simply said.

We left the noise and smell of the fishing harbour and headed towards to the town, stopping at a couple of tiny, bright blue painted stalls selling freshly squeezed orange juice, no machines here – the oranges were deftly juiced by hand as we waited. A nearby conch shell seller fussed over Charlie and Loli and fetched fresh water for them to drink. No hustle, just kind heartedness. As the last of the juice was supped, Chris and Jay hung their noses over a huge spider crab being sold by a man next to the stalls, it took Tina and Julie to point out that they didn't have a cooking pot big enough for it, to lure them away.

Into the old Medina, past another army of fresh fish vendors, this time offering their catch freshly cooked on the spot for you. Their stalls housed open grills which belched out clouds of smoke. The fresh, shining, and sometimes still moving, displays of the days catch were tempting, picnic tables loaded with sightseers gobbling up the seafood stood nearby. European faces openly drank beer in the streets, drawing our attention in the same way that a lady, on the beach in a bikini, had. Morocco seemed to become less Moroccan on the Atlantic coast.

We ate in a restaurant on the main square, a great place to people watch. Jay noticed a quadriplegic man painting pictures using his mouth. As he wondered how someone with such a disability survived here, a waiter took food to the artist. Laughing and joking in camaraderie as he cut it up and fed him, the Muslim values of looking each other still strong even in this most European of resorts.

Walking around the bustling medina, its narrow streets lined with shops, we could see why it's a UNESCO World Heritage listed city. Enveloping it, the thick protective walls of the fortress, topped with cannons, gave a sense of historic power. Artist's images of the city were lined up to sell next to the cannons along the tops of the walls, while the cool dark of the barrel-vaulted, low-ceilinged munitions and supply chambers built into the city's walls, were now filled with shops, galleries and even a spa.

The hundreds of shops in the medina were full of the same things we'd seen for sale all across Morocco, and almost every shop had a small corner selling items made from wood. Essaouira's craftsmen are renowned for their lacquer-ware. The forests around Essaouira are mostly Thuya woods, and the local craftsmen have made a name, and a living, producing items from it. The distinctive dark burled grain and fragrant aroma make it stand out from other woods and tourists flock in their thousands to snap up intricately inlaid boxes, chessboards and curios at very cheap prices. Julie was seriously tempted to buy a little box, but with space being at a premium in Dave she talked herself out of it. The town left us with a warm feeling, minimal hassle but still the hustle and bustle of a genuine, working port. It was going to be hard to tear ourselves away.

Back at the campsite the men gutted the sardines, feeding the unwanted innards to a myriad of cats. Tina prepared the red fish with lemon, bay leaves, butter and garlic and our gas BBQ cooked it all up a treat. An hour later we were all stuffed full of fish, as were Charlie, Loli and one of the campsite kittens, which had proved itself tougher than Charlie in a claws-out scrabble for dropped bits. It was a fitting feast for our last night with Chris and Tina as the following morning we had to bid farewell to them. Their insurance enabled them to stay in Morocco for three months, if ours did we'd be hard pushed to get out of Essaouira. As we could only stay for a month, we needed to make our way back towards the ferry port.

After a hugged farewell, knowing we'd see Chris and Tina again on another continent, we set off, heading north through an agricultural area, in a convoy of one. The rough eaten edge of tarmac dropped away into ploughed fields, patched together with lush green squares of crops or grass, we weren't sure which. Shin-high stone walls marked out the edge of some fields, tumbling apart in places, while other parcels of land were marked by nothing other than a change in colour. A car pulling a trailer packed with cows, people stood along the side of the road waiting for lifts and men struggling with wooden ploughs washed us of the feeling we'd perhaps left Morocco in the east. In an isolated spot, a chicken decided to play chicken with Dave, forcing us to pull over and check if it had embedded itself in something mechanically important. Through some luck, Insha'Allah perhaps, it had escaped. As we lifted our heads a rabble of nippers, arms outstretched, appeared in the distance, running towards us. With Dave's engine roaring, we too escaped.

Turning towards the coast, we drove through the resort of Safi on our way to our overnight stop at Oualidia. An Acima supermarket car park offered respite from the continual attempts to flag us down. For some reason supermarket car parks are like hallowed ground, and no-one would approach us while we were parked in them. Grabbing lunch, a cuppa and then a tank of filthy-cheap diesel we took to the road again. Young girls desperately thrust conches and necklaces of shells into the road as we passed and caught sight of the Atlantic again.

Finally, after several hours of driving, we reached Oualidia. Once called *Morocco's best-kept secret,* a phrase that surely dooms any unsuspecting off-the-beaten-track town to a future of intensive over-development, the fishing village is spread around a sheltered, sandy lagoon which teems with bird life. We turned off the main road and headed down a hill towards a European looking block paved square, behind which was a car park filled with motorhomes all under the watchful eye of a *Guardien,* in his obligatory high visibility jacket. A price list at the entrance tells us it's 25 Dirhams a night; perfect.

This was our first overnight Guarded Parking location, and we expected there to be some form of guarding going on. However, once we'd paid, high-vis man disappeared, leaving us to fend off seller after seller appearing at the window with bags and boxes of food. One chap even wandered about with his donkey. We guessed he was selling from packs on its back rather than attempting to offload the beast itself to a passing European punter.

Unable to face any more sellers, and in need of a leg stretch, we went for a walk. Across the decoratively paved square and concrete pavements shaped and coloured to look like wooden logs, a short path took us to a sandbank overlooking the huge lagoon. Blue wooden boats, covered to provide shade from the sun, waited to ferry people around the lagoon. Using one would give a closer view of the migrating egrets, herons, curlews and flamingos but we declined the inevitable offer from a hands-in-pocket man, sticking with our binoculars.

Ambling along in the bright sunlight we rounded a dune to find locals casting fishing lines off volcanic outcrops into the ocean. BBQs stood waist high on wooden poles and anything caught was roasted up on the spot for their families who sat close together under umbrellas. Charlie took full advantage of a discarded spider crab leg that was as long as he is tall, tilting his head to stop it from dragging in the sand as he walked. Eventually he found a suitable spot and lay in the sun and nibbled on it like a bread stick.

As the sun emitted the last light of the day, setting the sea on fire, it felt as if our Moroccan adventure was coming to an end. Oualidia was again unlike the Morocco we'd seen over the past few weeks. We'd read how its smart European styling attracts wealthy Moroccans and ex-pat French in high season earning it the dubious title of the *St Tropez of Morocco*, but in February it felt more like the *Newquay of Cornwall*. Lacking the dusty, crumbling, chaotic, and exotic souks and medinas, the shops sat perched up by the main road away from the beach. Walking around there was none of the standard come-inside-please-look-see-beautiful-handmade-Berber-carpet patter. There were no donkeys hurtling towards us with trailers in tow and very few of them on the roads, which were now wide, black strips of tarmac, had ever seen a rusting moped with an entire family perched on it. Would the rest of the coast be like this, easing us back into Europe? We worried how we would feel about the remainder of our European travels; would everywhere else seem bland and boring in comparison?

The following morning, taking the cowards approach and keeping our curtains shut until the last possible moment, we managed to avoid the attention of early-morning sellers. Today a decision needed to be made; between us and the port was Casablanca and Morocco's capital city Rabat. The thought of Rabat didn't lure us at all, we figured it would be like all other capital cities we've ever visited. But Casablanca, conjured up images of *Play it again Sam*, romance and black and white movies. Driving along the motorway we looked across to the city to see if we could see a hint of any of this, but our view was of high rise tower blocks, industrial units, advertising boards promoting diamond necklaces, Pizza Hut and McDonalds.

Wanting to remember Morocco as we'd seen it, donkeys, teleboutiques, djellabas, dark bustling souks and rivers being used for clothes washing, we decided to give Casablanca a miss too. We carried on along the wide, flat, smooth toll road, which was like any other motorway in Europe, but still held its own Moroccan quirkiness. People with donkeys wandered along on the other side of the fence, sheep grazed on the verges and at one point we passed four maintenance men clipping the hedges in the central reservation, with hand shears.

One thing which remained the same throughout our travels in this country: in reality, nothing was as close as it looked on a map. To reach Kenitra, the next campsite that we knew of after Rabat, took many more hours of solid driving.

The dusty, unkempt campsite and a walk around the town confirmed to us that Kenitra is not a typical destination for tourists. There was no medina, just modern block style concrete architecture, housing above; shops beneath. Many of the shops seemed to be selling old, broken or second-hand electronic items such as microwaves and kettles - we made a mental note to send 'kettle killer' Chris an email and let him know. No one tried to sell us things or entice us into their shop as we walked along. If it wasn't for Charlie, we would have been totally ignored.

Sitting on the edge of a fountain in the main town square, which flowed only with discarded rubbish, we stared at huge bags stuffed to bursting with wool. Fresh from a sheep, they were sat in a shop doorway, maybe waiting to be washed and spun, a faint smell of the countryside seeping from them. After Essaouira and Oualidia, Kenitra was a tired town, in need of a serious clean-up operation. It didn't have the excuse of crumbling city walls, the place was just dirty. For a country where very few people drink alcohol, the amount of broken glass in the streets was akin to what we'd expect to see in a British city early on a Sunday morning. Rubbish lined the gutters and edges of the pavement by the shop windows, Charlie had a field day, and we had a nightmare trying to keep him away from the chicken bones and mouldy bits of orange scatted around the place.

Even though it was filthy, there was, as always, plenty to see. Nothing seems to take place in private in Morocco as businesses operate with far less space, simply using the pavement and road as extended premises. Wandering along we watched butchers hack up meat and kill poultry in full public view, electricians fixing microwaves sat on stools in the street, carpenters making tables with sawdust blowing across the pavement and mechanics fixing cars in the road.

Finally it struck us. Kenitra is a town where people live normal lives, and they don't care about doing anything special to attract tourists. Maybe we had now found the real, true Morocco. If so, we didn't really think it was up to much. Perhaps we didn't find Kenitra's hidden wonders, but after seeing enough, we didn't feel like hunting any further, so made our way back to the campsite. Agreeing it was nothing more than a well positioned stop-over we envied a group of Italian bikers who had the right idea, they arrived late and leave early, we weren't that far behind them.

An hour further north and another 40 Dirhams in tolls we arrived at Moulay Bousselham, a town which is pretty much one street which ends at the sea. Driving along roads that were virtually our own, we passed women so heavily loaded that from a distance we thought they were donkeys. The campsite commands a prime position, situated on the edge of a massive lagoon. It's home to Merdja Zerga Biological Reserve, one of Morocco's most important wetlands and top birding destinations, and it made the lagoon at Oualidia look like a puddle.

By the campsite entrance fishermen were unloading their catch. Feeling brave after our fish buying in Essaouira we set off for a look to see what was on offer. As soon as we stepped foot over the campsite boundary we were approached by Khalil trying to sell us a tour in his boat around the lagoon for 300 Dirhams, which soon became 200 Dirhams when we looked uninterested. Knowing nothing about bird life, we really weren't interested, so thanked him and carried on to the fish fest. Jay went in for a closer look while Julie held Charlie back from scoffing everything in sight. Seizing his moment, Khalil joined Julie and after a bit of haggling we found ourselves agreeing to an hour long tour of the lagoon for 100 Dirhams.

Following our new-found and possibly faux-guide over to a flotilla of wooden boats with small motor engines, we waited while Khalil wandered off to fetch a bag containing two sets of well cared for high-powered binoculars and a bird spotting book. We wobbled onto the boat, Jay carrying Charlie on board, and settled in. Charlie lay glued to the floor of the boat, Khalil sat at the motor and pointed out birds, naming them all, no need for the book after all.

Khalil told us he'd been a bird guide for 20 years, since he gave up fishing, and that in December and January the wetland receives a population of at least 100,000 waterfowl of various species. There is also a good population of waders, including flamingos, little ringed plovers, black winged stilts and black tailed godwits. The names went over our heads, but Khalil obviously genuinely loves them, describing some as beautiful and pointing out those which are rare in the UK. We were happy to sit there and let him wax lyrical about all things feathered and his gite (guest house) next to the lagoon which he was trying to get into the Rough Guide to Morocco, the path to riches for a small business like his.

Back on dry land and with the end of our trip looming, Julie spent an hour cleaning more of the Sahara out of Dave, while Jay worked on oiling Dave's squeaking leaf springs, again, and extracting a small dead bird from the engine cover. Chores completed we treated ourselves to a takeaway of piping hot chips from the campsite restaurant, before an early night, as tomorrow we'd be facing Tangier.

THE LAST TANGO IN TANGIER

To many, Tangier marks the start of their Moroccan adventure, ferries sail into its port full of bemused tourists seeking a sense of the exotic in Africa. To us it marked the beginning of the end of our trip, it was our last port of call before we set sail back to Europe. We'd only been away a month, but it seemed far longer than that.

As we drove through Tangier we passed the usual Western big city icons, McDonalds; still identifiable even though its name was written in Arabic. Billboards lined the roads advertising printers, mobile phones and apartment complexes, all a far cry from watching a goat herder deciding whether or not to eat a bit of orange he'd found on the floor. The road took us through our nemesis, Tangier port. The thought of it scared us four weeks ago, so we'd avoided its chaos and touts by sailing into Tangier Med port further up the coast. After a month in the country we were more than ready to face it. Approaching its entrance, men stood by their little metal-box offices on the roadside waving, offering tickets. A month ago we'd have panicked, slowed down, worried what we needed to do; now we simply drove through the throng without batting an eyelid.

Just as we were starting to feel like seasoned travellers, the campsite tripped us up, locating itself half way up a steep hill approached by a couple of hairpin bends. Peering up the precipitous road as we drove past we figured that couldn't possibly be the place. We discovered it was, as the road we were on continued back into the city. Once more the road looked more treacherous than it actually was and on reaching the top we parked up Dave, on one of the lower levels, knowing we'd have to walk back up here later on.

Our adventure's end was to be suitably celebrated with a tagine in Tangier. Walking along the new coast road we wound our way up to the medina, which curiously contained maps and signs funded by the EU - perhaps it had lost far too many of its members citizens in the maze? We ignored the maps we wandered around soaking up the atmosphere. In 1923, Tangier became a destination for many European and American diplomats, spies, writers and businessmen, and we could see why. Its beautiful beaches entertain the sun worshippers while the old town has an enduring charm, a strong European influence taking the edge off the Moroccan rawness. Rows of shops offered traditional goods along with electronics, designer clothes and watches. The owners, selling the same items we'd seen a million times before, tried to entice us in, we simply smiled and with a causal wave of the hand walked on. There are so many lovely things we would buy if we were on a short trip, but as we looked at them we only saw storage problems and clutter in Dave for the next six months. Besides, we'd already collected a couple of Berber blankets, a cactus silk throw, a Djellaba, a Berber jacket, a box of dates and a camel made from a woven palm leaf. Knowing what persistent sellers the Moroccan people are, we think we got away lightly.

We walked up to the top of the medina walls and looked across the Gibraltar straight, the mountainous coast of Spain a grey outline in the distance. Below us work was taking place building a new part to the port, lorries carrying huge rocks made their way out along a causeway then dumped their cargo once they reached the end, slowly the causeway was extending. It all looked so simple, yet effective. We'd found that a lot in Morocco. Things could move on at a great pace, but people seem happy as they are. Mobile phones have been embraced, yet water still needs collecting from wells and clothes washed in rivers.

Hungry for a final feast, we stood looking at Café Colon, partly because we were both amused by the name and partly because we were unsure if it served food. A man approached us asking if we were looking to eat, when we said we were he told us he had a restaurant around the corner that we could go, as Café Colon only served drinks. We knew he was a tout, we knew he was probably lying about Café Colon, and we knew he didn't have a restaurant but would be paid by one he took us into, but we wanted one last fling, so we played along.

Making sure we agreed a price for our meal up front and knew exactly what was included we had already decided what we would have before we got there. Previous experience taught us there were only three main things on offer: tagine, cous-cous or kefta. Julie had eaten several kefta already, so opted for a chicken tagine while Jay had the cous-cous. To start with we both enjoyed a spicy Moroccan soup with bread. This was followed by a pastilla, a chicken or pigeon pie, depending on who you ask. The meat is mixed with nuts, wrapped in flaky pastry and sprinkled with icing sugar. It sounds unappetising, but is strangely tasty. We'd been curious about pastilla ever since Fes when the French couple touring with us had one for their lunch; that meal now felt like a lifetime ago. It was not only fitting that our

148

last meal was traditional food, but also that it was all so well done, and bought to us via a tout.

Said tout hung around during the meal and then took us to his *son's* herbalist shop, where his *son*, who unsurprisingly looked nothing like him, told us all about the different herbs and spices and what they are all used for. We thanked him for his time and left empty handed, there was simply nothing we wanted or needed. A few weeks ago we wouldn't dare enter a shop for fear of being sold to, now it was no longer a challenge to get out without buying something, perhaps it was a good time for us to leave, we were getting too used to the place.

Nevertheless, we had heavy hearts as we drove towards the ferry port the following day. Sure we were getting used to the place and there wasn't really so much of a challenge in it, but it was still so different. The people were so friendly and welcoming, and we felt safe.

Now knowing how long it takes to get from place to place, and remembering the time it took to get through customs and into the country, we set off at 11am for our 5pm ferry. As we drove along the coast road we laughed as how we felt when we arrived, too scared to stop or talk to people, worried by the men standing at the side of the road, unsure if we needed to stop or not at police roadblocks.

During our adventure we'd managed to trade a bike and dog carrier, barter with wine and beer and have a thoroughly good time. We were leaving with a few mementos and thousands of photos, but the main things we would leave with would be great memories and a new found respect for Moroccan people. The only thing left for us to do was to fill up with cheap diesel and drive past the touts lining the road to the ferry port.

Once in the port we knew how to play the game, our documents were only handed over once we'd identified our ferry company's representative, and another representative who spoke English told us of the process to get out. Pencils and Dirhams were exchanged for the information and soon we were back at the currency exchange portacabins. Julie handed over our remaining Dirhams and in return got a few Euro notes and a couple of Dirham coins, *"For next time"* the man behind the counter said smiling.

ABOUT THE AUTHORS

Julie and Jason Buckley, were both born in 1972 and grew up on opposite sides of Nottinghamshire. With a little help from their friends they met in a church, albeit one that had been converted into a bar, in 2003. Four years later they were married, four years after that they had saved up enough money to take a break from their corporate lives and travel.

Selling most of their possessions, and shoving what they couldn't fit in their ageing motorhome into willing family and friend's attics, they rented out their house. On the 12th October 2011 they crossed the English Channel to start their adventure.

Travelling through France, Northern Spain and Portugal they met like-minded couples and formed great friendships. A change to the Pet Passport scheme gave them the opportunity to visit Morocco, along with Charlie, their Cavalier King Charles Spaniel, so they took it.

By keeping to a budget and staying in cheap, or preferably free, places the couple have since managed to stretch out their savings to another year on the road. After returning to the UK for an MOT in September 2012, they set off again a couple of weeks later and are currently travelling around the continent, and eyeing up a trip to Tunisia!

They wrote this book while they travelled Europe. You can continue to follow their adventures on their website. They publish photos, videos and daily updates as they travel on www.ourtour.co.uk.

OTHER BOOKS BY THE AUTHORS

OurTour Guide to Motorhome Morocco

The perfect book to help you plan your own trip to Morocco and to give you a flavour of what to expect! The guide focuses on the practical, first hand experience we gained from taking Dave, our motorhome, and Charlie, our dog, to Morocco.

It covers topics such as: driving a motorhome in Morocco, a step-by-step guide to entering and leaving, what to take and what not to take, when to haggle and when not to, finding safe places to stay, scams and nuisances.

It also lists the campsites and guarded parking we used, and our thoughts about them.

OurTour Guide to Motorhome Morocco is available as an ebook on Amazon, or direct from our website OurTour.co.uk

3447832R00086

Printed in Great Britain
by Amazon.co.uk, Ltd.,
Marston Gate.